W9-ALN-956

THE BIG WORLD OF FUN FACTS

THE BIG WORLD OF FUN FACTS

JUMP-START YOUR CURIOSITY WITH THOUSANDS OF FUN FACTS!

H.W. POOLE

Published in November 2019 by Lonely Planet Global Ltd
CRN: 554153
ISBN: 9781788683333
www.lonelyplanetkids.com
© Lonely Planet 2019

ACKNOWLEDGMENTS
Developed by Print Matters Productions Inc
Author: H.W. Poole
Design: Tim Palin Creative
Photo Editor: Uliana Bazar
Publishing Director: Piers Pickard
Publisher: Hanna Otero
Art Director: Ryan Thomann
Commissioning Editor: Rhoda Belleza
Print Production: Lisa Ford

MIX
Paper from
responsible sources
FSC™ C021741

Paper in this book is certified against the
Forest Stewardship Council™ standards.
FSC™ promotes environmentally responsible,
socially beneficial and economically viable
management of the world's forests.

Printed in Malaysia
10 9 8 7 6 5 4 3 2 1

STAY IN TOUCH
lonelyplanet.com/contact

Lonely Planet Offices
AUSTRALIA The Malt Store, Level 3, 551 Swanston St, Carlton,
Victoria 3053 T: 03 8379 8000
IRELAND Digital Depot, Roe Lane (off Thomas St), Digital Hub, Dublin 8, D08 TCV4
USA 124 Linden St, Oakland, CA 94607
UK 240 Blackfriars Rd, London SE1 8NW

Contents

NATIONS OF THE WORLD

There are around 200 countries in the world, but getting an exact number is tricky because not everyone agrees about what qualifies as a country. **DO YOU NEED A FLAG TO BE A COUNTRY?** An anthem? **WHAT ABOUT MONEY**—does a country need its own currency to be considered a real country? This chapter looks at the symbolic side of national identity.

IT'S A GOOD IDEA to wear old clothes for the Hindu festival of Holi. A big part of the celebrations involves throwing brightly colored powder at your friends, smearing it all over, and throwing water balloons.

THE FIRST NATIONAL ANTHEM was Great Britain's "God Save the King," adopted in 1745. The anthem is adapted, depending on whether a king or queen sits on the throne.

SOME COUNTRIES OPT TO USE US DOLLARS instead of having their own currency. Ecuador, El Salvador, Palau, Timor-Leste, and Zimbabwe are just a few examples.

Superlatives

Most and least, biggest and smallest, oldest and newest . . . these countries top the lists.

SMALL ISLAND, SMALLER HOMES

Hong Kong (right) has the smallest average house size in the world. About 200,000 of its residents live in spaces called "coffin apartments" because that's literally how big they are. **A typical coffin apartment is about three feet by six feet (1 m by 2 m) and costs around US$310 per month.** Think about that—there are likely people you know who are too tall to fit in a coffin apartment.

THE RUSSIAN BEAR IS BIG

Russia (below) is the largest country in the world in terms of landmass: 6.6 million square miles (17.1 million sq km). Canada comes in second, with 3.9 million square miles (9.9 million sq km). If you were to shrink Russia's borders to make it the same size as Canada, the leftover land would, all by itself, constitute the world's seventh-largest country!

BATTLE OF THE TALL TOWERS

The record for the tallest building has been hard fought for thousands of years. The first "world's tallest" tower was the Tower of Jericho, built in what is now the West Bank around 8,000 BCE. It was only 28 feet (8.5 m) high, but it remained the world's biggest tower for thousands of years.

Modern architecture blew that record out of the water. In 1931, New York City's Empire State Building became the world's largest tower: it is 1,250 feet (381 m) tall, or 1,454 feet (443 m) if you include the giant antenna.

Then, in 1967, the title of tallest building was stolen by the Ostankino Tower, a radio and TV broadcasting tower in Moscow. Ostankino was outbuilt by the CN Tower in Toronto, and later by Taipei 101 in Taiwan. **Since 2010, the world's tallest tower has been the Burj Khalifa, in Dubai (below).** It is 2,716 feet (828 m) tall—that is, more than two Empire State Buildings!

MOST of the MOST

CHINA HAS THE LARGEST POPULATION: more than 1.38 billion in 2018. India is not far behind, with 1.29 billion.

THE MOST DENSELY POPULATED COUNTRY IS MONACO, with 37,000 people packed into 0.78 square miles (2 sq km).

THE BIGGEST CITY BY NUMBER OF PEOPLE IS TOKYO (below), with more than 38 million.

THE BIGGEST CITY BY LAND MASS is the New York metropolitan area.

National Wealth

Natural resources, such as minerals, forests, water, are the assets a country has to work with. Countries rise and fall based on how they manage their resources.

SITTING ON VOLCANOES

Almost all of Iceland's energy comes from renewable resources (right). But unlike most renewable energy, which comes from the sky in the form of sun or wind, Icelanders' power comes from below their feet. Because the country is located over a chain of active, below-ground volcanoes, Iceland has extremely good access to geothermal energy—the heat generated from inside the earth. **Ninety percent of homes in Iceland are heated with geothermal energy.**

THE TROUBLE WITH TANTALUM

Tantalum is an element used in the manufacture of capacitors (below), **tiny devices inside smart phones, computers, and gaming systems** that are essential to energy storage. Capacitors can be made from a number of different metals, but tantalum has proved particularly efficient. That's the good news.

The bad news is that nearly half of the world's tantalum supply comes from the Democratic Republic of the Congo, parts of which have been wracked by bloody civil war for decades. Unfortunately, many of the brutal warlords who terrorize the region fund their murderous activities with tantalum profits. That's why tantalum is known as a "conflict mineral." Public pressure in the West against enriching these murderous warlords has had an effect. In 2016, for example, Apple announced that its products were completely free of conflict minerals for the first time.

THERE'S (A LITTLE) GOLD IN THEM THAR HILLS

There's not as much gold (right) in the world as you probably think. By one estimate, if you were to gather up all the gold that's been mined in all of human history, you'd have enough to fill a little over three Olympic-sized swimming pools. Some of the top gold-mining operations include Muruntau (Uzbekistan), Grasberg (Indonesia), Pueblo Viejo (Dominican Republic), Yanacocha (Peru), and Goldstrike (Nevada, United States).

MINING DOWN UNDER

Aluminum is an extremely useful, readily available metal that can be easily recycled. In fact, a soda can (below) made from aluminum can be used, recycled, and back on the shelf as a new can in about 60 days. **About two-thirds of all the aluminum ever created is still in use today.**

The thing is, aluminum can't be mined; it has to be made from a mineral called bauxite. Australia, China, and Brazil are the world's top three bauxite-mining countries. Australia produces by far the most—more than 71,000 tons (65,000 metric tons) every year, which is nearly as much as China and Brazil combined. The countries of India, Guinea, and Jamaica also mine bauxite, but in far smaller amounts.

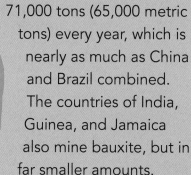

RESOURCE FACTS

RUSSIA HAS THE LARGEST AMOUNT OF NATURAL RESOURCES OVERALL—including the largest reserves of both coal and gold.

CANADA HAS THE LARGEST AMOUNT OF WATER OF ANY COUNTRY—almost 20 percent of the world's fresh water (above).

SURINAME HAS THE MOST TREES:

95 percent of the country is forested land.

YUMA, ARIZONA, IS CONSIDERED THE SUNNIEST PLACE ON EARTH, with more than 4,000 hours of sunshine every year.

You've Got to See It

The Eiffel Tower, the Taj Mahal, the Statue of Liberty . . . every country has its special places that are sources of pride and identity.

CAMELOT IS REAL

In northwest Ethiopia lies the ancient city of Gonder, a seat of power for more than 200 years (1632 to 1855). The emperors who ruled during that period constructed **spectacular castles (below) that look a bit like the homes of King Arthur and his Knights of the Round Table**, causing the city to be nicknamed the African Camelot. Unfortunately, many of the grand palaces, stables, and churches were destroyed when Ethiopia was occupied by Italy during World War II. The United Nations is in the process of helping to restore the ruins.

A VERY STYLISH STATUE

The year 2019 marks an impressive anniversary **in the city of Brussels, Belgium: a young boy will have been peeing in a fountain for 400 years.**

The brass statue, known as Manneken Pis (above), is only 24 inches (61 cm) high, but it looms large in the imaginations of the people of Belgium. Although the statue itself is nude, **Belgians make a game of creating costumes for the little boy**. Over the years the statue has worn the uniform of the national soccer team many times; he's also been dressed as a jazz musician, an Olympic skater, a jogger, a train conductor, Dracula, Nelson Mandela, and hundreds of other characters.

One yarn about the origins of the statue involves a wealthy tourist who visited Belgium with his family and lost track of his son; when the boy was eventually found peeing in a garden, the father supposedly had the statue made as a thank-you gift. In truth, there's no good answer to the question of why the little boy pees, just that he does and, one assumes, always will.

SCULPTURE FOR SCUBA

The Caribbean island nation of Grenada is home to **one of the world's most unique landmarks**: a sculpture park that's best seen while wearing scuba gear.

The Molinere Underwater Sculpture Park (right) was created by a British sculptor named Jason deCaires Taylor. Located about two miles off the coast, the park opened in 2006. The sculptures, all human figures cast in concrete, include a man sitting at a desk, another man riding a bike, and a group of young children holding hands. Over the years, sculptures by other artists have been added to the site.

In addition to being an amazing work of art and one of Grenada's proudest landmarks, the sculpture park has a second role—shoring up the country's coral reefs, which have been damaged by hurricanes.

ANCIENT ULURU

The sandstone rock formation of Uluru, also called Ayres Rock (left), stands as tall as a skyscraper in Australia's Northwest Territory. Uluru is 1,141 feet (348 m) tall—just a tad shorter than the Empire State Building—and its circumference is 5.8 miles (9.4 km). **It's considered sacred by the local indigenous people**, the Aṇangu, whose ancestors have lived in Central Australia for some 30,000 years. Caves inside Uluru feature Anangu art that's believed to be about 5,000 years old.

GIVE US A HUG

The most recognizable symbol of Rio de Janeiro is surely the **massive statue of Jesus (right) that looks down on the city** from the top of Mount Corcovado. Completed in 1931, the statue stands 98 feet (30 m) tall atop a pedestal that adds an additional 26 feet (8 m). And yet, it's not nearly the tallest statue of Christ in the world. There are statues in Vietnam, Poland, and Bolivia that are all bigger, while Mexico and Indonesia have statues that are roughly the same size.

Interestingly, **nearly all the statues feature Christ in the same open-armed posture**. Many assume the widespread arms signify his position on the cross, but not everyone in Rio agrees. In 1969, Brazilian musician Gilberto Gil wrote a song about the statue called "Aquele Abraço," which translates as "The Hug."

Raise It High

Flags have been used to declare a group's identity since at least the 1700s, and every nation on Earth has its own flag.

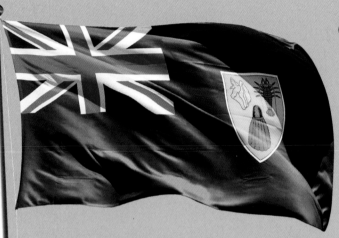

CLOSE ENOUGH?

The Turks and Caicos Islands are south of the Bahamas—not a place known for snow. **So how did an igloo end up on their flag?**

Because the main natural resource on the island is salt, an official badge of the island featured two white lumps, representing piles of salt ready for export. When the time came to create an official flag for the islands in 1899, the artist mistook the salt piles for human dwellings and drew a little door on one of them! And so it was that these tropical islands had what appeared to be an igloo on their flag. **The mistake wasn't rectified until 1968, when a conch shell and a lobster replaced the igloo (left).**

IN FINE SHAPE

What shape is a flag? Rectangular, right? All flags are rectangular. Well . . . not quite.

Switzerland and Vatican City both have square flags. **But the world's most unique flag shape is Nepal's: two overlapping triangles (right), one on top of the other.** The triangles are meant to represent both the Himalayan mountains and the two religions of Nepal: Hinduism and Buddhism. Legend has it that the Hindu god Vishnu presented the people of Nepal with the design of their flag. That may be so, but the design wasn't officially adopted until the year 1962.

A DECLARATION OF UPSIDE DOWN

The flag of the Philippines (right) was adopted when the country became independent from Spain in 1898. It's known as a bicolor, meaning that it's dominated by two stripes, in this case blue on the top and red on the bottom. But **when the country is at war, the flag is deliberately flown upside down**—the red stripe on the top lets everyone know that a battle is coming.

MY FLAG IS YOUR FLAG

The creation of Haiti's flag (below) involves an inspiring tale. In 1803 revolutionary leader Jean-Jacques Dessalines supposedly tore up a French tricolor flag, removed the white stripe in the middle, and instructed his daughter to sew the remaining blue and red stripes together. **The new flag symbolized the independence of people of color in Haiti from the white French.**

Imagine the Haitians' surprise when they arrived at the opening ceremonies of the 1936 Summer Olympics, only to discover that the tiny country of Liechtenstein had the identical flag. After the games, Liechtenstein added a golden crown to its flag, to make it unique. Haiti's current flag features a coat of arms in the middle of the two stripes.

FLAG FACTS

THE FLAG OF BELIZE IS THE ONLY ONE WITH IMAGES OF PEOPLE ON IT; two woodcutters standing beneath a tree.

NO COUNTRY uses the color purple in its flag.

DENMARK'S FLAG IS RED WITH A WHITE CROSS, and it was adopted in the 1300s. It's usually cited as the world's oldest continuously used flag.

THE US FLAG ON THE MOON appears to be waving even though there's no gravity and no wind. The flag was equipped with a little mechanical arm that was meant to hold the flag straight out at a 90-degree angle. But the arm doesn't work! So the flag, which was intended to look flat, instead looks rumpled in photos.

THE EXPLORER SIR EDMUND HILLARY AND SHERPA TENZING NORGAY were the first to plant a flag at the top of Mount Everest. Hillary was a New Zealander and Norgay was Nepalese, but they had to use a British flag because Great Britain had paid for their trip.

Sing It Loud

The first national anthem was Great Britain's "God Save the King," adopted in 1745. Ever since, national anthems have been important symbols of national identity.

A SHORT ONE

When Uganda was founded in 1962, **a contest was held to determine the new country's anthem**. The government specified that it wanted the anthem to be "short, original, solemn, praising, and looking toward the future." Many entries were submitted, and the anthem committee chose . . . none of them—they disliked them all! Instead, they threw out the entries and hired a professor named George Kakoma to write the song. In one day, Professor Kakoma came up with a lovely piece that's only nine measures long—one of the shortest anthems in the world.

SAME OLD SONG

One of the world's older anthems belongs, fittingly, to one of the world's oldest countries: Japan. The lyrics of "Kimi Ga Yo" (The Emperor's Reign) come from poetry written in the 10th century. Interestingly, although "Kimi Ga Yo" has been an important part of Japan's national life for centuries, it didn't become the official anthem until 1999, when the country finally passed a law recognizing its official symbols.

NOTHING TO SING HERE

Afghanistan had no anthem at all for about a decade. The country had been taken over by a group of violent Muslim extremists called the Taliban, and the new regime made all music illegal. After they were overthrown in 2001, a new constitution was put into place that called for a new anthem. It took time, but in May 2006 the country adopted a newly composed anthem with the toe-tapping title of **"Allah Soroud-e-Melli-e Da Afġānistān Islāmī Jomhoriyat" (National Anthem of the Islamic Republic of Afghanistan).**

BUT WHO GETS TO KEEP THE DOG?

The anthems of eastern European countries Slovakia and the Czech Republic are the result of a forced marriage followed by a peaceful divorce.

In 1918, a new nation was created from the ruins of World War I. Territories held by people known as the Czechs were knitted together with territories of the Slovaks, creating Czechoslovakia. To please both sides, the new nation's anthem took one section from a song called **"Where Is My Home?"** from a Czech opera, and one section from a popular Slovak song, **"Lightning Over the Tatras."**

In the 1990s, countries across eastern Europe were declaring their independence, and Czechoslovakia was no different. The country was split into the Czech Republic and Slovakia in 1993, and each side took its half of the anthem with it.

ANTHEMS FROM AROUND THE WORLD

ANGOLA: "Angola Avante" (Forward Angola)

BAHAMAS: "March On, Bahamaland"

BHUTAN: "Druk Tsendhen" (Thunder Dragon Kingdom)

CHAD: "La Tchadienne" (People of Chad)

EGYPT: "Bilady, Bilady, Bilady" (My Country, My Country, My Country)

GEORGIA: "Tavisupleba" (Freedom)

INDIA: "Jana Gana Mana" (Hail the Ruler of All Minds)

KIRIBATI: "Teirake Kaini Kiribati" (Stand Up, Kiribati)

MYANMAR: "Kaba Ma Kyei" (Till the End of the World)

PAPUA NEW GUINEA: "O Arise, All You Sons"

RWANDA: "Rwanda Nziza" (Beautiful Rwanda)

SOUTH SUDAN: "South Sudan Oyee!" (South Sudan, Hooray!)

TONGA: "Ko e fasi 'o e tu'l 'o e 'Otu Tonga" (Song of the King of the Tonga Islands)

UKRAINE: "Shche ne Vmerla Ukrania" (Ukraine's Glory Has Not Perished)

ZAMBIA: "Stand and Sing of Zambia, Proud and Free"

Counting Coins

They say money makes the world go around, and there's a lot to learn about money around the world.

CAN YOU SPARE A TRILLION?

What's the largest denomination of paper money you've ever seen, a $100 bill? That's the largest type circulated in the United States these days. What do you think a $1 trillion bill would look like?

During a 2009 economic crisis in Zimbabwe, **one US dollar was worth $2,621,984,228, 675,650,147,435,579,309** in Zimbabwean dollars. The government was forced to issue a trillion-dollar bill (ZWD$1,000, 000,000,000). But inflation was so bad, even the trillion-dollar bill quickly became useless— it wasn't even worth enough to pay for bus fare. Zimbabwe soon switched its economy to using South African and US currency (below) instead.

OKAY, YOU WON

Dealing with money in the two Koreas has been a bewildering business at times. South and North Korea both call their currency the "won," but that's where the similarity ends: the two currencies are totally different, and they have different values.

Complicating matters, **North Korea (right) used to issue different currency for foreigners than it did for citizens.** But not only that: North Korea also had different currency for foreigners from socialist countries versus foreigners from capitalist countries. A visitor from, say, China, would use red won, while a visitor from the United States would have to use blue. Certain shops would only take local currency, while others would only take red and others blue. Around the turn of the 21st century, North Korea got rid of both red and blue wons, but visitors *still* aren't allowed to use the local money. It'll be dollars or credit only, 부디 (please).

HAVEN'T I SEEN YOU SOMEWHERE BEFORE?

It didn't become common to put human faces on coins until after the death of Alexander the Great in 323 BCE. By the time of the Roman Empire, getting their portrait on a coin was a top priority for every incoming emperor. Rome's holdings were so vast that a coin was the only picture of their leader that many citizens would ever see. Some of the short-lived Roman leaders are now referred to as "coin emperors," because they held power for such a brief time that getting their faces on coins are the only accomplishments historians can recall.

FREE MONEY?

Currency and country have been intertwined for thousands of years, but with the invention of cryptocurrency, that's beginning to change. **Cryptocurrencies**, which only exist in digital form, **have no connection to any specific economy or banking system.** The most famous are BitCoin (right) and Ethereum, but there are hundreds of others. These days, anyone with technical know-how can issue their own currency. **Some of the stranger ones include DentaCoin (for dentists), InsaneCoin, Mooncoin, Putincoin, Trumpcoin, and Unobtainium.**

MONEY FACTS

THE FIRST COINS WERE ISSUED IN LYDIA (today, western Turkey) by King Croesus in the sixth century BCE. Croesus, who was so rich that his very name became synonymous with amazing wealth, issued coins of pure gold and pure silver.

PAPER MONEY WAS INVENTED IN CHINA IN 806, where it was nicknamed "flying money" because it was so easy to lose.

SILVER AND GOLD COINS featuring Pokémon, Disney, and Star Wars characters are issued on Niue, a tiny island country near New Zealand. The coins are for collectors and not intended to be used. But they are legal tender, so in theory you *could* go shopping with Stormtrooper coins.

£1 MILLION AND £100 MILLION NOTES—nicknamed "the giant" and "the titan," respectively—actually exist in Great Britain. They are kept locked in a safe, providing insurance for deposits at Britain's banks.

This Means Us

How do Brazilians show pride in Brazil, Egyptians in Egypt, or Aussies in Australia? Sometimes it's through the display of their favorite national symbols.

ARE YOU FOR REAL?

Many countries choose a particular national animal because it's frequently seen within that country and has a strong association with the place. **The national animal of Australia is the kangaroo (right)**—of course it is, because where else would you see one? But not every country interprets "national animal" in such a literal way. Some countries' national animals have never been seen at all. The following are some of the more whimsical national animals:

- Czech Republic: Double-tailed lion
- Greece: Phoenix
- Scotland: Unicorn
- Mauritius: Dodo (the dodo isn't fictional, but it's been extinct since the 1600s!)
- North Korea: Chollima (a wild, winged horse from Chinese mythology)
- Wales: Y Ddraig Goch (Welsh dragon)

COUNTRIES IN ACCORD(ION)

Unlike, say, the "national animal," the "national instrument" of most countries is usually unofficial, but many countries have one nonetheless. And **there's one instrument that a surprising number of countries all claim as their own.** It's louder than a guitar and more portable than a piano: it's the accordion (left). The folk music of both Serbia and Slovenia is heavy on the accordion. The national instruments of Argentina and Russia, the bandoneon and the garmon, are small accordions with buttons instead of keys. The norteño style of music from northern Mexico is also accordion dependent, as is cumbia music in Colombia. You can't escape the accordion in Irish traditional music, or in Cajun and zydeco music from Louisiana and west Texas. And we can't forget the polka stylings of the Czech Republic, Germany, Poland, and many other countries. According to one report, **even North Korea has decreed the accordion to be "the people's instrument."**

SAY IT TO MY FACE

How powerful is a motto? **In 18th-century France, just three words—*liberté, égalité, fraternité* (liberty, equality, brotherhood) symbolized by the goddess of liberty (below)—kicked off a revolution** and later inspired a second revolution in Haiti, which took the phrase as its motto, too. Not every country has an official motto, but here is a global sampling of some that do.

- Bahamas: Forward, Onward, Upward Together
- Cuba: Patria o Muerte, Venceremos! (Homeland or Death, We Shall Overcome!)
- Saudi Arabia: Lā ʾilāha illā l-Lāh; Muḥammadu r-rasūlu l-Lāh (There Is No God Other Than God; Allah Is His Prophet)
- Spain: Plus Ultra (Further Beyond)
- Uruguay: Libertad o Muerte (Liberty or Death)
- Vietnam: Độc lập, Tự do, Hạnh phúc (Independence, Freedom, Happiness)

SYMBOL FACTS

THE NATIONAL BIRD OF BELIZE is a rainforest dweller called the keel-billed toucan. Toucans (right) are understood to be loyal, social, and devoted to family—all traits that Belizeans embrace as important to their national character.

THE UNOFFICIAL NATIONAL PLANT OF MALI IS COTTON—it is called "white gold" by locals because cotton is such an important contributor to the national economy.

INDONESIA'S NATIONAL ANIMAL IS THE DEADLY KOMODO DRAGON. Nicknamed "land alligators," the existence of komodos wasn't confirmed by Western scientists until 1926.

NATURE

Our planet supports an almost unimaginable diversity of life, and every country has its own UNIQUE, AMAZING, and sometimes DOWNRIGHT BIZARRE natural features.

AT THE TOP of the **East Antarctic Plateau**, temperatures can drop as low as **−148 degrees Fahrenheit** (−100°C). Scientists believe that's as cold as it's possible for Earth to get.

THE HOTTEST PLACE on the planet is a desert in Iran called **Dasht-e-Lut** ("Emptiness Plain") (left), where temperatures of **159.3 degrees Fahrenheit** (70.7°C) have been recorded.

Those who explored Dasht-e-Lut—the hottest place on the planet—expecting an abiotic (without life) environment, were surprised to find insects, reptiles, and even foxes that prowl the desert at night.

Cool Critters

Just as countries have their own interesting geography, biomes, and weather, they have their own fascinating animals, too.

WHEN PIGS SWIM

Who doesn't dream of running away to an exotic island with white sand beaches and azure waters and lots of pigs? (Oh, just me?)

Big Major Cay (right and below) is **an island in the Bahamas that's better known as Pig Beach (or Pig Island) because only wild pigs live there**. We don't know how they ended up on Big Major Cay. Maybe they swam there after a shipwreck, or maybe they were brought by humans and abandoned. Pig Beach is now a popular tourist attraction—excursions leave daily from Nassau. **The pigs are friendly, and they're happy to be fed by visitors**; they especially love carrots and grapes.

YOU'RE MAKING THAT UP

Australia's platypus (right) is the world's most confusing creature: a venomous, egg-laying mammal with the bill of a duck and the tail of a beaver. When the platypus was first displayed to European scientists in the early 1800s, most of them were sure it was a hoax. In the first-ever description of a platypus, naturalist George Shaw wrote, **"I almost doubt the testimony of my own eyes."**

FLAMINGO LAKES

Kenya's Lake Nakuru National Park (above) is **famous for its flamingos, which visit the lake in mind-blowing numbers**—as many as two million, or about a third of the global flamingo population! **They're attracted by the delicious blue-green algae on Lake Nakuru.** Recently, flooding diluted the saltiness of the lake, which reduced the algae. Many of the flamingos left for Lake Bogoria in Tanzania. The good news is, the algae has been gradually coming back, tempting flamingos to return.

BANKING ON BANKHAR

Mongolia is home to wandering herders, who raise sheep and goats all across the Mongol Steppe. The Steppe is an unforgiving environment; predators like snow leopards and wolves can easily destroy a nomad's herd. **A long time ago, a type of guardian dog called Bankhar (for "flat face") lived and worked among nomads, protecting the flocks.** The Bankhar (left) were nearly wiped out during the Soviet occupation. But the Mongolian Bankhar Dog Project is working to breed, raise, and place Bankhars with Mongolian herders. Evidence shows that Bankhars reduce attacks on livestock by 80 to 100 percent.

A KILLER CUTIE

The slow loris (right) is an adorable but potentially deadly animal native to Indonesia, Vietnam, and other parts of Southeast Asia. **The slow loris is equipped with a venom that can cause a severe allergic reaction in humans.** Odder still, the venom is located in its arms—when threatened, the loris licks its armpits, mixing the venom with saliva to create a poisonous brew.

You might have seen some "loris tickling" videos on the Internet. The clips seem fun, but the lorises in those videos are not having any fun at all. First, lorises are nocturnal, and the camera lights hurt their eyes. Second, lorises raise their arms in the air, not because they are being tickled, but because **they feel threatened . . . and are seriously considering poisoning you**.

Creepy Crawlies

Tiny bugs and microbes have an outsized impact on life on Earth.

THE LITTLEST HELPERS

Microbes (right) can improve and even save lives under the right circumstances.

- **PENICILLIN**, an antibiotic, is created by a mold called penicillium (in the genus *Penicillium*). It was discovered accidentally by Scottish scientist Alexander Fleming, who later wrote, "One sometimes finds what one is not looking for."
- **ZOMBIE ANT FUNGUS** infects an ant's brain, forcing it to bite down on a leaf that will help the fungus reproduce itself. Then the ant dies, and the fungus escapes through the ant's head.
- **MICROBES** are central to cleaning up oil spills. *Alcanivorax borkumensis* is one of several microbes that eats hydrocarbons.

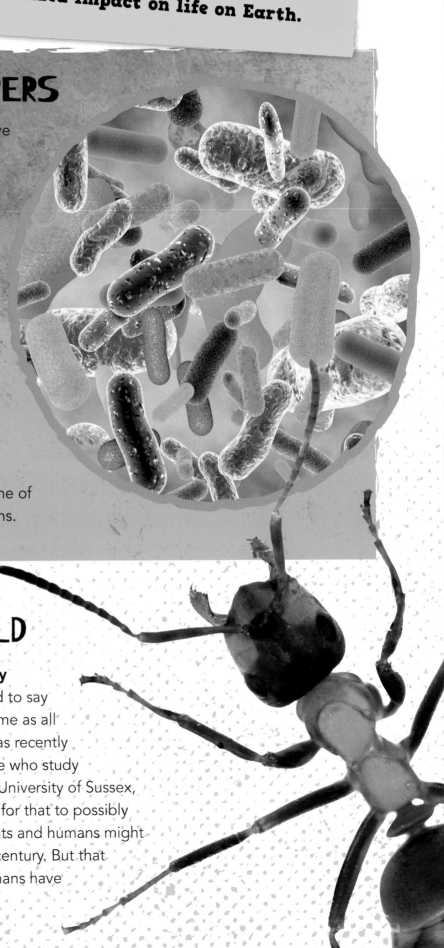

THE WEIGHT OF THE (ANT) WORLD

We share our planet with approximately 100,000 trillion ants (right). People used to say that all the ants in the world weigh the same as all the humans in the world, but that claim has recently been disputed by myrmecologists (people who study ants). Francis Ratnieks, a professor at the University of Sussex, argues that there are now too many of us for that to possibly be true. He believes that the totality of ants and humans might have weighed the same in, say, the 18th century. But that at 7 billion humans and counting, we humans have outweighed ants for some time.

THE SERIAL KILLERS OF SUMMER

Picture **the deadliest creature in the world**. What did you think of first? Maybe lions or sharks? Or maybe humans? No, the biggest killer is the tiny mosquito (above), which **kills some 750,000 people per year**. West Nile virus, yellow fever, and dengue fever are just a few of the serious diseases you can get from a mosquito bite. More than half of all mosquito-related fatalities are due to malaria, which is caused by parasites that hitch a ride in the female *Anopheles* mosquito. Malaria can occur anywhere the weather is warm enough to support this species, from sub-Saharan Africa to India, and from northern South America to Indonesia.

THE TITAN BEETLE

Titanus giganteus (above) can grow larger than an adult's hand, it has jaws that are strong enough to break a pencil, and, yes, it can fly.

DUNG BEETLES HAVE

been deliberately introduced to parts of Australia and South Africa in order to counteract the negative environmental impacts of cow dung on ranches.

THE KILLER BEE is a type

of honeybee bred by humans in Brazil. The scientists weren't trying to make a meaner honeybee, just a more productive one. But they were a bit too successful. Killer bees have killed around 1,000 people since escaping the lab in 1957.

Lay of the Land

The favorite catchphrase of the real estate business is "location, location, location," meaning *where* a home is can be just as significant as what it is. That can also be true for countries—location is everything.

CIUDAD SINKING

Mexico City (below) sits in a basin in the central part of the country, surrounded by mountains. Its main water supply is the massive aquifers (underground lakes) right underneath the city. As the population passes well over 8 million, the city is removing water from the aquifers faster than they can be refilled. Underground water levels are dropping at just over three feet (1 m) per year, and that's having a big impact on the architecture of Mexico City itself. **The city has sunk more than 30 feet (9 m) since the 1950s.** Streets are buckling, buildings are leaning, and pipes are bursting—one estimate suggests that as much as 40 percent of the city's water is wasted on leaks.

IT'S NOT LOGICAL, CAPTAIN

It's a tiny island in a tiny lake, on a small island in a small lake, all on a larger island. There's also a volcano involved. Welcome to Vulcan Point (below)—it's not logical.

Let's start at the beginning. **The Philippines is a collection of more than 7,000 islands in Southeast Asia.** One of those islands is called Luzon, and it has a lake called Lake Taal. Sitting in the middle of Lake Taal (right) is an active volcano, which is called Taal Volcano, or simply Volcano Island. Sitting on the volcano, about 1,000 feet (304 m) up, is Main Crater Lake. And within that lake is a little nubbin of land called Vulcan Point, also known as the island in a lake on an island in a lake on an island.

ALL MAPS ARE WRONG

The map of the world you probably know is called a Mercator projection (below); it's based on the work of Gerardus Mercator from the mid-1500s and shows the round world in a distorted, flattened form. Mercator's map is good for indicating location—where one place is in relation to another place. But it's weaker when it comes to the size of one place in relation to another.

The most infamous Mercator misstep is Greenland; it's not, in fact, the same size as the continent of Africa—NOT EVEN CLOSE. Speaking of Africa, Mercator's map doesn't give a good sense of how big that continent really is. The United States, China, India, Japan, and most of Europe could all fit within Africa.

REAL PLACE NAME FACTS

Welcome to
DULL
Paired with Boring, Oregon, USA
Drive Safely

- Buttock Point, Isle of Bute, Scotland
- Catbrain, South Gloucestershire, England
- Ding Dong, Texas, United States
- Executive Committee Range, Antarctica
- Gogogogo, Ampanihy, Madagascar
- Head-Smashed-In Buffalo Jump, Alberta, Canada
- Idiotville, Oregon, United States
- Monster, South Holland, Netherlands
- Mount Disappointment, Perth, Australia
- Pity Me, Durham, England
- Saint-Louis-de-Ha-Ha!, Quebec, Canada
- Silly, Sissili, Burkina Faso
- Taumata whakatangi hangakoauau o tamatea turi pukakapiki maunga horo nuku pokai whenua kitanatahu, New Zealand

Life as We Know It

Ecosystems are complex communities of animals, plants, and other life forms that depend on one another for survival.

THE URBAN JUNGLE

With every passing year, we are turning more "wild" ecosystems into urban ones. **About 55 percent of the world's population lives in an urban area—** the United Nations projects that it will increase to 68 percent by 2050.

But just because people move in, it doesn't mean that the plants and animals go away: successful species adapt. For example, bird songs in urban environments are louder and more high-pitched than the songs of the exact same types of birds in other ecosystems. Birds adapt their songs to the noise level of their environment.

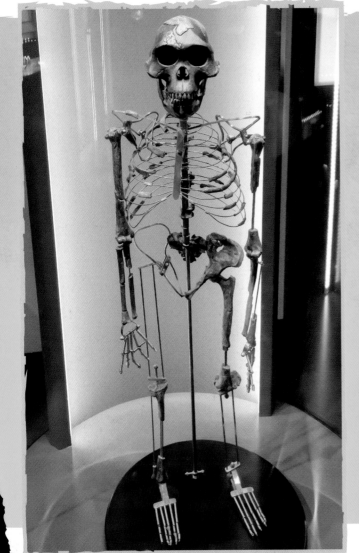

THE CRUELEST PLACE

The countries of Eritrea and Ethiopia share an ecosystem called the Danakil Depression, which a *National Geographic* writer once referred to as "the cruelest place on Earth." The Danakil Depression has an average temperature of 93.2 degrees Fahrenheit (34°C). It's home to hydrothermal vents and hot springs, vast salt flats, boiling chemical lakes, and an active volcano called Erta Ale. And yet, despite the inhospitable surroundings, **the Danakil Depression is also where archaeologists found the fossilized skeleton called Lucy (left), one of our most ancient ancestors.**

BIOME FACTS

THE WORLD'S LARGEST ECOSYSTEM is the taiga, also called the boreal forest or snow forest. Vast stretches of taiga can be found across northern Europe and Asia. North America also has its own taiga, all across Canada and Alaska.

In dense, **TROPICAL RAINFORESTS** it's estimated that only about 2 percent of sunlight actually reaches the ground.

FREEZING IN THE DESERT

Not all deserts are hot: there are cold deserts that also have very little rain. **One of the best-known is the Gobi Desert in China and Mongolia (above), where winter temperatures can get as low as −40 degrees Fahrenheit (−40°C).** In summer, temperatures can climb to 113 degrees Fahrenheit (45° C). Other cold deserts can be found in Greenland, Iran, Chile, and, surprisingly, even in a part of southern Africa, where the cold ocean current prevents rain, creating the Namib Cold Desert. Many scientists also consider Antarctica to be a "cold desert"—although others refer to it as a "polar desert" instead.

CORAL ECOSYSTEMS PROVIDE HABITATS TO ABOUT A QUARTER OF ALL MARINE SPECIES.
They're critical parts of the marine ecosystem, but most coral reefs (above) are struggling to survive in increasingly warm waters. **We have lost about half of our coral reefs since the mid-1980s**, and may lose about 90 percent by 2050.

Off the Beaten Path

The big blue marble we all call home is also home to some amazing, and amazingly strange, natural phenomena.

CATHEDRAL OF MARBLE

The Cuevas de Mármol (Marble Caves) of Chile (right) are on Lake General Carrera, near the Argentine border. Over thousands of years, the water has carved spectacular caves into the calcium carbonate cliffs. **The caves themselves are actually white and gray, but the reflections of the lake's azure water can make them appear different shades of blue and green.** One cave in particular is so remarkable it's known as the Marble Cathedral.

WORLD'S SMALLEST DESERT—OR IS IT?

Only one square mile (2.2 sq km) in size, the Carcross Desert (below) in Yukon, Canada, is known as the world's smallest desert. It was created by a glacier about 12,000 years ago. Of course, some critics complain that, given the natural humidity in that part of Canada, Carcross isn't dry enough to qualify as a true desert. These killjoys say Carcross is better described as a collection of sand dunes.

In any case, Carcross Desert (yeah, I said it!) is located along the Alaska Highway just south of Whitehorse. It's a popular spot for sandboarding in summer and snowboarding in winter.

WALKING ON THE MOON

On the Greek island of Milos (right) is a beach called Sarakiniko, where the winds and waves have formed the white volcanic cliffs into amazing shapes. **Sarakiniko is often called "the moon beach"** because of its otherworldly landscape. Carved beneath the rock is a network of abandoned mines, where Ancient Greeks used to dig for minerals and sulphur.

ISLANDS IN THE SKY

When we think about ecosystems, we tend to think horizontally. But did you know that some ecosystems are stacked vertically?

Sky islands are mountains that have markedly different ecosystems at their peaks than they do at the ground level. The term was first used to describe the Chiricahua mountain range in Arizona. The bottom of the mountain range has desert-like conditions, with hot, dry summers and mild winters. Meanwhile, more than 9,000 feet up, it's colder and wetter—the top of the mountains receive about twice as much precipitation as the bottom.

There are sky islands all over the world: Mount Kilimanjaro in Tanzania (below); Mount Wilhelm in Papua New Guinea; Yushan (or Jade Mountain) in China; Sierra de Tamaulipas in Mexico; Baikal Mountains in Siberia, and the Altai Mountains, a range that spreads across Mongolia, Kazakhstan, Russia, and China—and that's naming just a few!

Today's Forecast

The author Mark Twain once wrote that "climate is what we expect; weather is what we get." But some of the world's climates are anything but expected.

THE LIGHTHOUSE OF CATATUMBO

Whoever said "lightning doesn't strike twice" never saw the Catatumbo River in Venezuela. In the northwestern part of the country, where the river flows into Lake Maracaibo, regular, **massive lightning storms (right) happen every night for about eight months out of the year.** Lasting up to 10 hours each time, the storms can be seen from about 250 miles (400 km) away—ship captains in the region used to use the Catatumbo lightning to guide their ships at night. It's said that the explorer Sir Francis Drake was foiled in his attempt to invade this part of Venezuela because the lightning revealed the positions of his men.

GATEWAY TO THE SNOW?

The town of Aïn Séfra, Algeria (below), is sometimes called the "gateway to the Sahara," and as such it is one of the hottest places on Earth. The record temperature for the month of July is 107.4 degrees Fahrenheit (41.9°C) and for August is 109.2 degrees Fahrenheit (42.9°C). Imagine their surprise in January 2018 when **townspeople looked outside to see a blanket of snow!**

Actually, their surprise might not have been quite what you'd think, since it also snowed in 2017. That storm was even bigger, dumping as much as three feet (1 m) in some spots. It was the first snow that Aïn Séfra had seen since the late 1970s.

A RED RAIN IS GONNA FALL

In the Ancient Greek poem *The Iliad* by Homer, the god Zeus (right) causes the clouds to rain blood on several occasions—a pretty dramatic way to get a message across.

When "blood rain" occurred in Kerala, India, in 2001, scientists were able to study the phenomenon and get some answers. **Kerala's blood rain was caused by algae in the genus *Trentepohlia*,** which grows on tree bark. Other colored rains—which can be red, yellow, green, or even black—have occurred in other parts of the world. Some of these incidents are caused by algae, others by dust particles, but none, so far as we know, can be ascribed to Zeus being angry with us.

WATCH YOUR HEAD

High up in the Himalayan mountains, in the Indian state of Uttarakhand, there's a small glacial lake called Roopkund. The locals have a different name for it: Skeleton Lake.

This extremely remote body of water was discovered by a park ranger in 1942. The lake itself is not really what grabbed his attention, but rather the hundreds of skeletons surrounding it.

For many years, no one could figure out what had killed all these people. Eventually, it was learned that the people all died at once, back in the ninth century. It wasn't war, illness, starvation, or some grim mass suicide. **No, it was killer hail (above). A sudden, violent hailstorm flung chunks of ice the size of tennis balls from the sky, and around 300 people died of their head injuries.** Some of the skeletons remain there today, alongside their stone spears and leather shoes.

DRAGON'S TWISTS

When a fire rages, it doesn't just burn whatever is around; it also heats up the air very quickly. This fast-rising air can begin to rotate, causing what is sometimes called a **"fire tornado" (below).** These events are not technically tornados, however; scientists prefer the term **"fire whirl,"** to distinguish them as unique events. A 2018 forest fire in Carr, California, caused a fire whirl so large that it showed up on Doppler weather radar, and it did look like a tornado made of fire.

In September 1923, an earthquake south of Tokyo was followed by a fire whirl that grew to 300 feet (91 m) tall. Close to half of the entire city of Tokyo was burned by what locals referred to as "a dragon's twist," and about 45,000 people died in the flames.

Rooted or Not

Plants can be food, and they can be medicine. Some can declare love and others hate, and there's even a plant that's nearly immortal.

FARTS.
IT'S WHAT'S FOR DINNER.

Next time somebody tells you to eat your spinach, be glad they didn't say, "Eat your petai." **Petai (right) are the broad, flat beans produced by the plant *Parkia speciosa*.** They are eaten all over South Asia, including Malaysia, Singapore, Indonesia, and Thailand, where they're called "sato." Petai beans are full of nutrition, but their smell is similar to methane, which is to say rotten eggs or sewer gas. Yes, petai beans are nicknamed "stink beans" because, let's not mince words here, **they smell like farts.**

SOCOTRA, MOTHER OF DRAGON TREES

Socotra Island, in the Indian Ocean, is part of Yemen. Because the island is quite isolated, much of its plant and animal life can be found nowhere else in the world.

Archaeologists have found evidence of an ancient city on Socotra, but these days it's home mainly to shipwrecks and some very alien-looking plant life. **The dragon blood tree (right) grows a broad canopy to shade its roots from the hot sun.** Its name comes from the fact that if you cut into the tree, **it "bleeds" a bright red sap.**

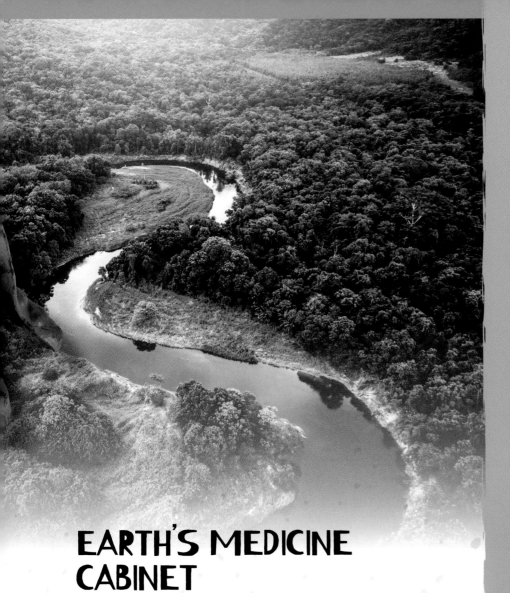

EARTH'S MEDICINE CABINET

There are an estimated 150,000 species of plants in the Amazon rainforest (above). Everyone from traditional healers to pharmaceutical labs wants to know about the potential healing properties of what grows in the jungle. Here are a few intriguing ones:

- About 70 percent of all plants known to have cancer-fighting properties are found in the Amazon rainforests.
- It's believed that the sodo plant can cure addiction to both cigarettes and alcohol.
- The first medicine to effectively treat malaria was quinine, which was originally made from the cinchona tree bark by the Quechua people of Peru and Bolivia. Today, it also flavors tonic water.
- Indigenous warriors used to dip their arrowheads in a poison that they made from a climbing vine. Today, that poison is called tubocurarine, and it can be used (in safe doses) as a muscle relaxant and to treat tetanus and black widow spider bites.

FLOWER FACTS

IN RUSSIA, ROMANIA, SPAIN, and some other European countries, flowers are always given with an odd number of blooms because that's considered lucky . . . except never 13 blooms, yikes!

IN BELARUS, yellow flowers suggest either death or infidelity.

IN LATVIA, red roses aren't for romance, but for funerals.

IN JAPAN, *hanakotoba* is a complex "language of flowers": peonies are for bravery and zinnias for loyalty, while orange lilies whisper of hatred and vengeance.

DON'T OFFEND AN ITALIAN HOSTESS with a hydrangea, which are said to indicate a cold personality.

GOVERNMENT, POLITICS, AND THE LAW

Ever since the Code of Hammurabi, **the world's oldest surviving laws**, people have been trying to work out the best ways to organize governments, write laws, and, when needed, **PUNISH THOSE WHO VIOLATE THOSE LAWS.**

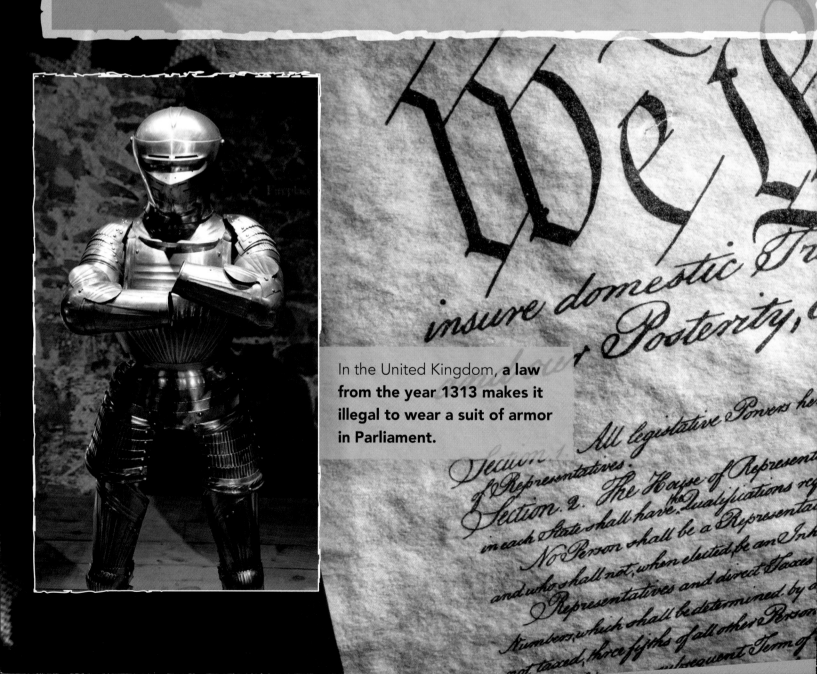

In the United Kingdom, **a law from the year 1313 makes it illegal to wear a suit of armor in Parliament.**

In China, State Religious Affairs Bureau Order #5 states that no one may be reincarnated without official government permission. What's more, anyone who is reincarnated must register and receive a special ID card.

The world's oldest surviving laws were inscribed on a seven-foot (2.1 m) stone pillar (right); they're known as the **CODE OF HAMMURABI**, after the Babylonian king who created the laws.

By the People, for the People?

From democracy to dictatorship and everything in between, there are lots of different ways to run a country.

IT'S MY PARTY

The US, UK, and Australian governments are called "two-party systems" because they have two main political parties. Lots of other governments don't work this way.

North Korea, for instance, has only one political party: the Korean Workers' Party (KWP). Technically there are two others, but they are controlled by the KWP. The situation in Syria is similar. Ruled for decades by the Ba'ath Party, Syria has other parties in theory, but the purpose of the other parties is to create an illusion that Syria is a democracy when it isn't. On the other hand, **about 200 political parties have had candidates run for office in Israel since that country was founded in 1948**. That's a small number compared to India (above), which has more than 2,000 political parties!

WHAT'S IN A NAME?

Slightly over half of the world's countries are constitutional democracies, where people vote for their leaders. **There are also monarchies and dictatorships, where the people get no choice about their leaders.** Here are some other terms used to describe types of government:

- **Isocracy:** government in which every citizen has an equal amount of political power
- **Kakistocracy:** government by the worst or least-qualified people
- **Kleptocracy:** government focused primarily on theft and corruption
- **Plantocracy:** government made up of plantation owners (also called slavocracy, after the plantation workforce)
- **Plutocracy:** government by the wealthiest citizens only
- **Technocracy:** government by a small group of technology experts
- **Timocracy:** a government in which you must be a landowner to participate (not, alas, a government run by people named Tim)

ANOTHER COUNTRY HEARD FROM

On July 4, 1964, Leicester Hemingway, brother of the famous author Ernest, set sail from Jamaica on a bamboo raft. He landed on a small island and declared it the country of New Atlantis. The country had seven citizens, and they elected Leicester as their first president. "There's no law that says you can't start your own country," he told a reporter, and he was right. **These self-declared "countries" are called micronations, but they're almost never recognized in any kind of official way.** The following are just a few examples:

- Republic of Molossia (within the United States)
- Principality of Sealand (offshore of Great Britain)
- Principality of Hutt River (within Australia)
- Empire of Atlantium (within Australia)
- Republic of Whangamomona (within New Zealand)
- Free Republic of Alcatraz (within Italy)
- Akhzivland (within Israel)

Who's in Charge?

It's good to be the boss . . . most of the time.

"FIRST" LADIES

The first female prime minister was Sirimavo Bandaranaike of Sri Lanka (then called Ceylon) in 1960. Six years later, nearby India chose Indira Gandhi as prime minister. Golda Meir became prime minister of Israel in 1969. Two more firsts followed, when Isabel Peron was appointed Argentina's first female president in 1974, and the following year Elisabeth Domitien was appointed the first female president of the Central African Republic. **Next was Margaret Thatcher (left), who became prime minister of Great Britain in 1979.**

NICE WORK IF YOU CAN GET IT

King Mswati III of eSwatini (formerly Swaziland), in southern Africa, is **the world's last remaining absolute monarch**. He, his 15 wives, and his 30 children live a very lavish lifestyle—the annual royal budget is US$61 million. That attracts a lot of criticism in a country where 60 percent of the population lives on US$2 per day, many in simple huts (above).

WE DON'T LOOK UP TO YOU

When a short man has a big attitude, he's said to have a "Napoleon complex," in honor of Emperor Napoleon Bonaparte (right). But despite the fact that Napoleon has a complex named after him, **historians now believe Napoleon was actually five feet six inches (1.68 m) tall. That's not towering, but it's not remarkably short either.** Both Vladimir Lenin and Joseph Stalin were an inch shorter than Napoleon. North Korean dictator Kim Jong-il was only five feet three inches (1.60 m), as was the terrifying Nikita Khrushchev, leader of the Soviet Union in the 1960s. Yasser Arafat, longtime leader of the Palestine Liberation Organization, was only five feet two inches (1.57 m), the same height as Iranian president Mahmoud Ahmadinejad.

Napoleon's height was actually a pretty good height for a leader. After all, **Alexander the Great and Winston Churchill were also five feet six inches (1.68 m).**

THEY USED TO BE INTERESTING PEOPLE

Things don't always end well for strongmen. Shortly after the Allied Powers defeated Italy in World War II, Italian dictator Benito Mussolini (below) said, "Seven years ago, I was an interesting person; now I am a corpse." At the time, he was speaking metaphorically . . . but not for long. Just a few months later, Benito and his mistress were shot and hung by their feet in a public square in Milan.

Brutal Romanian dictator Nikolae Ceauşescu and his wife left this planet in much the same way. After losing control of their country in 1989, **they fled the capital of Bucharest but were quickly captured by the army and executed**.

Muammar Gaddafi of Libya was likewise caught while trying to flee the country he'd terrorized for decades. He was beaten, dragged around, poked with knives, and finally shot in the head. Then his body was put in a freezer and displayed to the public for several days.

The People Speak

Voting is the duty of every citizen, but not every country does it the same way.

WHAT DAY IS IT?

In many English-speaking countries, it's common to hold elections during the week. Canadians expect to vote on Mondays, Americans on Tuesdays, and Brits on Thursdays. But in Australia and New Zealand, elections are usually held on Saturdays. Their weekend tradition is actually closer to most non-English-speaking parts of the world. **The most common day to have an election, according to the rest of the world, is Sunday.**

LOST YOUR MARBLES

The small African country of Gambia doesn't use paper ballots for voting. Instead, glass marbles (below) are rolled down chutes. Every time a vote is cast, a bell rings. The bells are a sort of safeguard so that poll workers know the machine is functioning correctly—and also that a voter hasn't rolled two marbles instead of one.

Voting with round objects might sound odd to those of us who are used to paper ballots, but it has a long history. **The Ancient Greeks often voted with pebbles**; voters would place their stones in the urn that represented their choice. The very word "ballot" comes from the French, *ballote*, which means small stone.

GET OUT THE (OUT-OF-THIS-WORLD) VOTE

People make lots of excuses why they can't get around to voting—bad weather, too busy, and so on. But few have as good an excuse as an astronaut aboard a space station.

In 1997 the state of Texas (home to a significant number of American astronauts) passed a law permitting Americans to cast their votes from space. The law was sponsored by a state senator who had won his election by only seven votes, so he knew all too well that every ballot counts. If an American astronaut is in space on Election Day, an encrypted ballot is emailed to him or her, and the astronaut fills out the ballot and emails it back. David Wolf was the first American to vote from space, while serving on the Russian space station *Mir*.

NAILED IT

Indonesia was run by the dictator General Suharto from 1967 to 1998. He and his party won every election, mainly because they murdered most of their political opponents.

The country adopted a process of voting using carpentry nails: voters would poke a hole in the photo of the candidate they wanted (right). The problem (or, if you are Suharto, the upside) was that the ballots were incredibly easy to manipulate. All poll workers had to do was poke a second hole to make the entire ballot invalid, so it would be thrown out.

Now that Suharto is gone, some Indonesians want to get rid of the voting method that's so associated with his regime. In the 2004 and 2008 elections, attempts were made to switch to paper voting. But the switch didn't go well—too many people used the pen to poke holes in the ballot instead of writing. For now, at least, the nail-poke tradition remains.

Defending the Nation

Most countries have some sort of military to defend their borders, but they're all run in different ways.

BUILDING A FORCE BY FORCE

There are roughly 60 countries in the world with compulsory military service, where young men (and sometimes women) are required to spend a certain amount of time serving in their country's military.

- Brazil demands 10 to 12 months of service from all 18-year-old males.
- Eritrea expects young men and women to serve for 18 months. If they are not needed in the military, they are given civilian jobs instead. Unfortunately, the service can drag on long past the 18-month mark—even lasting decades.
- Israel expects men to serve for three years and women for two.
- North Korea requires 10 years of service from men and seven from women; people with college degrees serve "only" five years, and those with degrees in scientific fields are allowed to skate by with only three years.
- Switzerland demands 21 weeks of service from men; Swiss women don't have to serve, but they can choose to do so.

BLINK AND YOU MISS IT

The shortest military conflict on record took place on August 27, 1896, between Great Britain and the Sultanate of Zanzibar (now the Tanzanian archipelago, in eastern Africa).

The sultan of Zanzibar, Hamad bin Thuwaini, died on August 25—he was probably murdered by his cousin Khalid bin Barghash. Khalid thought this was the perfect moment to make himself sultan, but let's just say the Brits disagreed. The British began shelling the palace (left) at 9:02 a.m. on the 27th. It took Khalid roughly 38 minutes to see the light: the Anglo-Zanzibar war was over at 9:40.

WHAT'S FOR DINNER?

When armies are on the move, and kitchens are a distant fantasy, soldiers often depend on field rations, also called MREs (meals ready to eat) (below).

Every country's military designs its MREs differently. **Indonesian MREs come with a tiny mobile stove, fuel tablets, and matches** so that you can heat up your meal no matter where you are. Italian MREs don't have stoves, but they do come with **toothbrushes and toothpicks**. MREs include classic flavors from the home country: **barbecue sauce** for American soldiers, **Vegemite** for Australians, **kimchi** for South Koreans.

At Bagram Air Force Base in Afghanistan, home to an international coalition of soldiers, it's common for people to swap their MREs for those from other countries. Not all MREs are created equal: at Bagram, the going rate was five American MREs in exchange for just one from France.

BIG AND SMALL

According to the International Institute for Strategic Studies, the five largest militaries (based on number of active-duty personnel) are as follows:

- China: 2,035,000 on active duty
- India: 1,395,100 on active duty
- United States: 1,348,000 on active duty
- North Korea: 1,280,000 on active duty
- Russia: 900,000 on active duty

The five smallest are

- Gambia: 800 on active duty
- Barbados: 620 on active duty
- Seychelles: 420 on active duty
- Antigua and Barbuda: 180 on active duty
- Haiti: 150 on active duty

Just Don't Do It

Nations express their priorities through what they make legal or illegal. Some countries have interesting . . . priorities!

GOLDFISH GET LONELY TOO

In 2008, the Swiss government passed a very thorough animal-protection law. The law has detailed rules pertaining to specific types of pets. All dog owners must take a pet-care class at their own expense, for instance. All guinea pig owners must have cages of a certain minimum size. **You can't own just one goldfish (right); you must always have at least two, so that the fish don't get lonely.** The same goes for parrots—you can't own just one. When it comes to cats, you are allowed to have just one, but only if you let it go outside to hang out with its kitty friends.

GHOST LICENSES?

In China, State Religious Affairs Bureau Order #5 states that no one may be reincarnated without official government permission. What's more, anyone who is reincarnated must register and receive a special ID card. What is this about? It's about Tibet.

Tibet is a region of China that has long resisted Chinese control. To Tibetans, **their most important political and religious leader is the Dalai Llama**. Tibetan Buddhists value the teachings of Buddha (left) and believe that each new Dalai Llama is a reincarnation of a previous one. It's not just the top guy, either—other high-ranking Buddhist leaders are also believed to be reincarnations of previous ones.

China's Order #5 sounds goofy, but it may in fact be an attempt to wrest control over Tibetan Buddhism in general and the Dalai Llama in particular.

HANDS OFF OUR SPUDS

In the state of Western Australia, **it's illegal to own too many potatoes (above).** The law was inspired by Australian potato farmers' desire to limit imports—the fewer potatoes there are, the more their own potatoes are worth. The limit is set at 110 pounds (50 kg), which admittedly is enough for quite a few fries!

DEATH TAKES A HOLIDAY

In 2000, the mayor of Le Lavandou, a small town on the French Riviera (below), passed a law banning death. **Yes, it became illegal for anyone to die in Le Lavandou.** The law was passed in response to the mayor's battle with the regional planning commission, which kept refusing permission to build a new and much-needed cemetery for Le Lavandou. Although it got the town some publicity, the law hasn't had much impact. "People die nonetheless," the mayor told a reporter. "It's terrible."

LAW FACTS

IN SWITZERLAND, it's illegal to flush the toilet after 10 p.m. because it's considered noise pollution.

IN SAMOA, it is illegal to forget your wife's birthday.

IN THE UNITED ARAB EMIRATES, you can be sent to jail for kissing in public.

IN MALAYSIA, owning a satellite dish that gets foreign television can earn you a steep fine, equivalent to hundreds of thousands of dollars.

Crime Doesn't Pay

You won't believe what some folks will do to skirt the law.

DEAR KIND SIR OR MADAM...

In 2016, an email from Dr. Bakare Tunde begged for help on behalf of his relative, Major Abacha Tunde. Major Tunde was the first African in space, but according to the email he'd been abandoned on a top-secret Soviet space station. The email went on to promise that he had a lot of money that he'd love to share with whomever would help him get back to Earth.

If this sounds dubious to you, and if you suspect that no such person exists, congratulations—**you've avoided a Nigerian email scam**. These scams are updates of the Spanish Prisoner, a con that dates back to the mid-1800s. In the Spanish Prisoner, a wealthy prince has supposedly been kidnapped, and his family will gratefully share their riches with you, if only you'll help fund his rescue. Another term for this nonsense is "advance-fee fraud."

Nigerian con artists are often accused of having invented the email version of the Spanish Prisoner. But in fact, they're just really good at it. The reality is that just as many "Nigerian emails" originate from the United States as from Nigeria.

MY PRECIOUSSSSS

Turkey's constitution has a provision that would be unthinkable to people in Western democracies. Provision 301 states that "publicly denigrating" state officials is punishable by two years in prison.

In 2015, President Recep Tayyip Erdoğan's feelings were hurt by a Facebook post comparing images of the president with Gollum (left), a character in J.R.R. Tolkien's *Lord of the Rings*. The poster, a doctor named Bilgin Çiftçi, was arrested and charged with violating Provision 301.

Çiftci's defense team assembled a panel of Tolkien experts to testify that the faces were not Gollum at all, but Smeagol, Gollum's "joyful, sweet" alter ego. They argued that since Smeagol is not evil, the Facebook post could not constitute "denigration" of Erdoğan.

In a victory for fantasy fans the world over, Çiftci was finally acquitted in 2017.

THIS FOOD IS DOWNRIGHT CRIMINAL

China is home to a lucrative (if icky) meat-smuggling industry. Chinese people eat increasing amounts of meat every year, and Chinese farmers are having trouble keeping up. Imports are strictly controlled, and US meat is banned entirely. So, criminal gangs try to meet consumer demand when farmers can't.

In 2015, smugglers were arrested for trying to sell 110,000 tons (100,000 metric tons) of **illegal frozen meat** (below) in several parts of the country. The shipments had a street value approaching US$500 million, despite the fact that much of the product was 40 years old and rotten.

"There was a whole truck of it," one official told reporters. **"It was smelly, and I nearly threw up when I opened the door."**

Far sweeter was the most valuable heist in Canadian history, involving that most Canadian of food items—maple syrup. Employees of the Federation of Quebec Maple Syrup Producers planned a theft that poured out slowly over 2011 and 2012. They siphoned syrup from storage barrels, replacing it with water, and then smuggled that stolen sweetness to sell in Vermont.

The heist was discovered when an inspector climbed on top of some of the barrels and they fell over. Water-filled barrels are lighter—and far less stable!—than syrup-filled ones.

Does the Punishment Fit?

Every country punishes crime in its own way. Did these "bad guys" get what they deserved?

CRUEL AND UNUSUAL AMPUTATIONS

Amputation has been used as a punishment for theft since ancient times. It's still used today, particularly in countries with hardline Muslim governments, such as Iran, Nigeria, Saudi Arabia, Somalia, Sudan, Syria, and Yemen. First-time offenders lose one hand, and repeat offenders risk losing the other, or even a leg. One specific practice is called cross-amputation: the accused loses a hand on one side of the body and a foot on the opposite side.

THE LONELIEST CONVICT

According to *World Prison Brief* from the Institute for Criminal Policy Research, **in 2018 the countries with the lowest number of prisoners were San Marino (2 inmates), Liechtenstein (10), Tuvalu (11), and Nauru (14).**

Having two prisoners in San Marino is actually a big increase—in 2011, the UK's *Daily Telegraph* reported only one person in jail in San Marino. The man's name was withheld for privacy reasons, so he became known as "the loneliest prisoner in the world." Since his sentence was only eight months, he's presumably been released by now; it's unlikely he got time added to his sentence for fighting with fellow inmates!

TROTSKY SLEPT HERE

Kresty Prison (below) in St. Petersburg, Russia, was built in 1730, but originally it stored wine, not inmates. Kresty was first used as a prison in 1867, and it became infamous for housing political prisoners—**the revolutionary leader Leon Trotksy is probably Kresty's best-known inmate.** The prisoners were all freed during the 1917 revolution, and they set fire to all the records before they left. Today, Kresty Prison is a museum honoring the building's history, and a new prison was built just outside of St. Petersburg. Nicknamed Kresty-2, **the facility was designed to house 4,000 inmates, making it the largest prison in Europe.**

IKEA PRISON

Norway is often cited as having the world's most effective prison system, due to its low rate of recidivism (meaning, when someone reoffends and has to go back to jail). **Only one-fifth of Norwegian ex-cons end up back in jail.** Compare that to the United States, where about two-thirds of released prisoners end up rearrested.

Norway has a number of so-called open prisons, which allow convicts to go to jobs outside and return to the prison after work. Inmates at Bastoy Prison, located on a small island, take a boat back and forth from work to jail. The facility houses 115 prisoners, many of whom are violent offenders, and yet it only needs three overnight guards. **Bastoy has been nicknamed "the IKEA prison" because the furniture in cells looks like it was bought at the popular Swedish furniture store.** (Ironically, the IKEA corporation had to issue a formal apology for using actual prisoners to build its furniture in the 1980s.)

PEOPLE AND CULTURE

WHAT MARKS YOU AS A MEMBER OF YOUR COMMUNITY? Is it your birthplace? Your family? Is it how you speak or what you wear? **People all over the world have different and fascinating answers.**

The women of the Mursi tribe in Ethiopia are known for their extraordinary *dhebi a tugoin*: large, flat discs that are inserted into their lower lips (left).

Girls of the Derung ethnic group in China (below) used to have designs tattooed onto their faces with sharpened bamboo—the tradition probably began as a way to discourage neighboring tribes from kidnapping the girls as slaves.

Who Are You?

Depending on your definition, there are between 13,000 and 24,000 ethnicities, or ethnic groups, in the world.

CHINA'S SMALLEST MINORITY

China has 56 recognized ethnic groups—some argue there are even more than that. The smallest minority group lives in northeast China. They're sometimes referred to as Nanai, which means "locals" or "natives," but they prefer the name Hezhen (right), which means "people of the eastern lower reaches."

In the 1700s there were about 50,000 Hezhen, but by 1945 there were only about 300 Hezhen remaining. The Hezhen, like other ethnic minorities, were exempted from China's one-child-per-family policy, first instituted in 1979. Instead, because of their dwindling numbers, the Hezhen, as well as other ethnic minorities and families living in rural areas, are encouraged to have as many as three children per family. This has resulted in a gradual but steady increase in the population, which is now approaching 5,000.

MESOAMERICAN MAYA

The Maya civilization in Mesoamerica dates back to around 1800 BCE and lasted until around 900 CE. The Maya are remembered for their writing system, their calendar and understanding of math, and their artwork and architecture. But it's not just their remarkable pyramids (below) that have survived—the Maya are also a contemporary ethnic group in Mexico and Central America.

Today there are between 5 and 6 million people with Mayan ancestry, speaking around 30 different Mayan languages (most Maya are bilingual and also speak Spanish). Mayan subgroups include the Yucatecs, who live on Mexico's Yucatan peninsula, the Quiché of Guatemala, and the Kekchi Maya of Belize. The smallest and arguably most threatened group of Maya are the Lacandon, who live deep in the Lacandon rainforest in Chiapas, Mexico. There are 300 or fewer Lacandon left.

A DIVERSE SUBCONTINENT

India is the second-most-populated country in the world and is often called the most diverse country on Earth. About two-thirds of the people are considered Indo-Aryan, but **there are also hundreds of ethnic groups**, subgroups, and tribes, speaking hundreds of different languages and dialects. There are Bengalis, Dalit, Dravidians, Kannada, Jat, Naga, Marathi, Parsi, Punjabis, Sindhis, Tamils, and many more.

THE SAN WERE FIRST

The Kalahari desert in southern Africa is home to the San people (below), sometimes referred to as Bushmen. An indigenous group of nomadic hunter-gatherers, **the San were probably the first inhabitants of what's now Botswana and South Africa**. Unfortunately, traditional San culture is dying out. As part of government-mandated "modernization" programs from the 1950s to the 1990s, the San were kicked off increasingly large areas of land and forced to become farmers. Some of the old ways can be seen in the hit 1980 film, *The Gods Must Be Crazy*. Namibian actor N!xau plays Xi, a San hunter, who encounters his first bit of modernity in the form of a Coca-Cola bottle that falls out of a plane.

We Need to Talk

There are about 7,000 languages spoken on Earth. Let's get to know our talkative world.

SCANDINAVIAN TRANSLATION

Each of the four Scandinavian countries has its own language—Swedish, Danish, Norwegian, and Finnish. The first three are closely related; someone who speaks Swedish has a good shot at understanding Danish and vice versa. That is absolutely not true when it comes to Finnish. **Finnish is actually more closely related to Estonian than to its Scandinavian neighbors.**

AN ANCIENT TONGUE

The Basque language is spoken in Basque country, located in Europe's Pyrenees mountain range, along the border between France and Spain. What makes the language so fascinating is that although Basque speakers (left) are geographically close to both French and Spanish speakers, their language bears no connection to either one. **Basque is all that remains of European languages that existed in the region before it became part of the Roman Empire.**

OLD FRIENDS

Although Spanish is the common language of Mexico, **the country is also home to 68 different indigenous languages**. Náhuatl has the largest number of speakers, with about 1.4 million. In the state of Tabasco, a language called Ayapaneco is spoken by only two men, Manuel Segovia and Isidro Velazquez. Making matters worse, the men had a falling out some years ago and stopped speaking to one another entirely! But in 2014, Segovia and Velazquez made up. They now run a school that teaches kids the Ayapaneco language.

LANGUAGE FACTS

THE ARCHI LANGUAGE is spoken in a small number of villages in Russia, near the Caspian Sea. Archi **has four genders instead of two**, and it has many more verb forms than we're used to. For instance, there's one verb to use when you're saying something you believe, and a slightly separate form to use if you are saying something you doubt.

THE AFRIKAANS LANGUAGE evolved from Dutch settlers who moved to South Africa. But the language has changed so much over time that contemporary speakers of Dutch and Afrikaans speakers can barely understand one another, if at all.

IN THE AMAZON RAINFOREST (below), a tribe called the Pirahã lives along the Maici River. Their language, also called Pirahã, has only **three pronouns, no past tense, no words for colors, and no numbers.**

That's a Mouthful

Here are some facts about words and choosing them carefully.

THERE'S ALWAYS SOMETHING GOOD AT THE KOPFKINO

One interesting feature of the German language is that it's very open to compound words. The result is that the German language offers some highly expressive, sometimes amazingly specific, terminology that you just can't find anywhere else. You may already know *weltschmerz*, which literally means "world hurt" and describes a nonspecific sadness that life stinks. Here are more **words found only in German**:

- *Fernweh* is a deep longing to be somewhere else.
- *Kopfkino* is the word for picturing a situation in your mind; it means **"head cinema."**
- *Torschlusspanik* is that creeping fear that you may not accomplish your goals before you run out of time.
- *Treppenwitz* literally means "staircase joke," and it refers to the clever comebacks that you think of after a conversation is over.
- *Verschlimmbessern* is the act of making something worse by trying to make it better.
- *Zechpreller* is a person who skips out on the check at a restaurant.

HUJAMBO, KISWAHILI?

With an estimated 100 million speakers, **Swahili (or Kiswahili) is the most-spoken language in Africa.** But there are only about 5 million native speakers. In the majority of cases, Swahili is a person's second (or third, or fourth) language. Like English, Swahili is a lingua franca, meaning it's a method of communication for people who speak different native languages.

DO YOU WANT THAT VODKA OR NOT?

In many languages, "Yes or no?" is a simple question with only two available answers. But Russians have a much more complex relationship to these apparently straightforward words. "Yes" in Russian is да (da) and "no" is нет, (nyet). But it does not end there, нет, нет, нет.

A common phrase in Russian is "да нет, наверное," (da nyet, navernoe), which can be translated as "yes no, maybe" or "yes no, probably." Basically, it's a soft no, along the lines of "not really" or "not exactly." **Your mom might say, "да нет, наверное" when you ask her for something and she kind of says yes but she actually means no.**

On the other hand, "ну, да" (nu, da) means "well, yes," and да, наверное" (da, navernoe) means "yes, maybe." Those are considered soft yeses—agreement is implied but not exactly definitive.

LANGUAGE FACTS

ALBANIANS HAVE 27 DIFFERENT WORDS FOR MOUSTACHES, and 27 other words for eyebrows.

IN SPANISH, the word *sobremesa* technically means "dessert," but what it actually means is that lovely period after a meal when everyone is sitting around chatting.

CWTCH is the longest word with no vowels; it's Welsh for "cuddle."

THE LONGEST WORD IN ENGLISH is the chemical name of a protein called *titin*. It **has 189,819 letters** and takes about three-and-a-half hours to pronounce!

As a Wise Person Once Said . . .

Proverbs are life-lessons in quotable form—pithy sayings that capture a fundamental truth about the world.

SAY UNTO OTHERS

There's a Cuban saying, **"When the sun rises, it rises for everyone."** That sounds like an ideal proverb for that country's collectivist mind-set.

But hang on a minute—is that really a Cuban saying, or did the Chinese say it first?

That's the thing about proverbs: people hear them, repeat them, translate them, adapt them. With the passage of time, it gets harder and harder to know where a particular saying began. By their very nature, proverbs belong to everyone.

Consider the so-called Golden Rule: "Do unto others as you would have them do unto you." Many people associate that saying with the Christian Bible, but it didn't start there. An ancient Egyptian tale called *The Eloquent Peasant*, dating back to the Middle Kingdom (2050 BCE to 1710 BCE) contains the same advice. Meanwhile, Buddhists, Hindus, Sikhs, Jews, Muslims, and Zoroastrians are all advised to follow roughly the same instruction.

LUCKY NUMBERS
9, 18, 99

Meals at Chinese restaurants generally end with a proverb that arrives at the table tucked into a cookie (below). But while fortune cookies are a staple of Chinese restaurants in Western countries, **they aren't Chinese in origin**. They were probably invented at a Japanese restaurant in San Francisco in the early 1900s; "probably" because there are numerous stories about where the cookies originated! In any case, fortune cookies are popular in Chinese restaurants all over the world *except* in China.

It's your lucky day

A PROVERB FOR PROTEST

Every great protest needs great signage. What better content for signs than proverbs, which distill the wisdom of the ages into a handful of words?

 "They tried to bury us; they didn't know we were seeds." Translated into Spanish, this saying was popularized at 2013 protests against the Mexican government. More recently it's been a common sight at US protests against the immigration policies of the Trump administration. The phrase is a reworked quote from a 1978 poem by a Greek writer, Dinos Christianopoulos. Ironically, Christianopoulos himself rarely stepped beyond his country's borders, while his words have traveled all over the world.

WISE WORDS

Japan: Fall seven times, stand up eight.

Spain: Whoever gossips to you will gossip about you.

Yoruba culture, Africa: Beheading is no cure for headaches.

Russia: There's no shame in not knowing; the shame lies in not finding out.

Sudan: A large chair does not make a king.

Denmark: Don't sail out farther than you can row back.

India: Life is a bridge: cross over it, but build no house on it.

Slovenia: Speak the truth, but leave immediately after. (Slovenia)

Argentina: The tongue of a false friend is sharper than a knife.

Ireland: Many's the time a man's mouth broke his nose.

Jamaica: Don't expect anything from a pig but a grunt.

Ethiopia: Evil enters like a needle but spreads like an oak tree.

Navajo: You can't wake someone who is pretending to be asleep.

Brazil: Strength is made by union.

Burkina Faso: You can't send a chicken to market if he knows he's the dish.

Australia: The bigger the hat, the smaller the property.

Norway: The bookless man is blind.

Just Don't Call Me "Late for Dinner"

What's in a name? As it turns out, quite a bit!

HEY, YOU

In Somalia, babies go without official names for the first 40 days of life.
Parents discuss naming ideas with family and friends, and they may consult their local imam (Islamic leader) as well. Parents often choose Muslim names, but they can select traditional Somali names if they prefer. After the 40 days have passed, a naming ceremony is held.

CAREFUL WITH KANJI

Japanese names are written with symbolic kanji characters (left) and given names can have between one and three kanji characters. Kanji can be tricky, however—**the same symbol can have different meanings, depending on context or on how the character is written**.
Sometimes Westerners try to write their names in kanji form by picking characters that roughly sound like their names, but this can be a mistake. For instance, the name Chris could be written as 躯里子. Spoken aloud (*kurisu*), it sounds a bit like the English name, but the symbols translate as "corpse foster child," which was probably not what poor old Chris was going for.

SON OR DÓTTIR?

Most Icelandic surnames are based on the person's father's name (or occasionally the mother's name), with "-son" added for boys and "-dóttir" added for girls. For example, the president of Iceland is Guðni Jóhannesson, which means he is Guðni, son of Jóhannes. In the 2016 election, one of the candidates he defeated was Halla Tómasdóttir, which means Halla, daughter of Tómas. Meanwhile, a popular Icelandic football player is called Heiðar Helguson, or Heiðar, son of Helga. From time to time, someone will have it both ways, as does the politician Dagur Bergþóruson Eggertsson; he is Dagur, son of Bergþóra (his mother) and son of Eggert (his father).

Iceland doesn't have the equivalent of "Mr." or "Mrs."—people are just referred to by their first names. Even the Icelandic phone book lists everyone alphabetically by first name.

NO NO, NABI

A typical Saudi Arabian name consists of a given name, the father's name, the grandfather's name, and the family name, which usually comes from the person's tribe. But in general, Saudis don't use all those names all the time. In day-to-day life, people are usually referred to by just their first name or their first name and surname.

Parents can choose their child's first name, but the government has a role, too. Western names like Linda are banned, for example. Also banned are names that are considered to be blasphemous: parents can't name their children Malak (angel), Nabi (prophet), or Tabarak (blessed). **The name Abdul is fine, but Abdul Nasser is forbidden, because the original Nasser helped overthrow the monarchy of Egypt in 1952.** Binyamin is also outlawed—possibly because of the name's association with Israeli politician Binyamin (Benjamin) Netanyahu.

Stories That Explain Us

A culture's folklore can tell you a lot about its people—what they value, what they celebrate, and even what they fear.

THE RIVER MAIDEN AND THE GOLDEN TABLE

Jamaica's River Mumma (River Maiden) is a bit like a mermaid—she appears to be human but can vanish into water in a flash. **The River Mumma can live in any large body of water, and all the fish are her children.** In some stories, she guards a solid gold table. There are tales of people trying to steal it, but the River Mumma pulls all of them into the water and drowns them. The lesson is, don't be greedy or the River Mumma will get you.

CAN'T CATCH ME

Saci Pererê (right) is a sometimes lovable, sometimes evil figure in Brazilian folklore. Whenever a toy goes missing, an egg doesn't hatch, or the milk goes bad, the mischievous Saci is probably to blame. Saci is a pipe-smoking, elflike character; he has only one leg, due to an **ill-fated capoeira fight**. If you are very lucky, you might catch Saci and keep him in a bottle. A captured Saci will grant you wishes, but treat him well, because if you are mean to him, he'll become your mortal enemy once he (inevitably) escapes.

THANKS FOR NOTHING, WAK

The Afars of Djibouti in East Africa (below) are Muslims today, but their folklore retains some elements of their pre-Islamic history, such as a fairly grim story about the beginnings of the world. According to the story, **Wak, the sky god who was the creator of everything, instructed Man to build his own coffin.** Man did so, and Wak promptly shut Man in it and rained fire down on him for seven years. Once the years had passed, Man was released from the coffin into the new world that Wak had created. But Man soon grew lonely, and so Wak took some of Man's blood and turned it into Woman. They had 30 children together— too many, apparently, because Wak took half and turned them into animals and demons.

BEWARE THE TIC POLONGA

People in Sri Lanka, an island country in the Indian Ocean, take their snakes very seriously. There are nearly 100 different species of snakes on the island, and about 30 of those are venemous. Some snakes are loved by Sri Lankans. **Cobras (right) are believed to be the reincarnations of dead relatives**, and it's considered fortunate to find one. But others are greatly feared. The worst of the lot is called the tic polonga (in the West it's called Russell's viper). **In Sri Lanka it's said that a tic polonga can live for 200 or more years.** When it is about to die, it supposedly grows a pair of wings and soars into the air, and anyone touched by its wings will immediately die. According to legend, in one final evil gesture, a dying tic polonga's body will burst open, showering the ground with scorpions, venemous spiders, and centipedes.

Clothes Make the Man (and Woman)

Jeans and sneakers may have almost conquered the world, but in lots of places around the world, fashion is closer to home.

HERERO

The Herero are an indigenous people in southern Africa, mainly Namibia and Botswana. The women wear long-sleeved, heavy dresses (right), which may seem surprising given the climate. The look is a holdover from the 19th century, when the region was controlled by the German Empire. The Germans insisted that the Herero people dress "modestly" and in accordance with Victorian values of the time.

Herero women today continue to dress in that style. But they don't do this because they fondly remember the Germans, who put the Herero into concentration camps and wiped out about three-quarters of the population. Instead, Herero women dress as they do to **honor the way their ancestors rebuilt their communities** *after* the Germans were kicked out. Today, they use fabrics and colors that are more African in style than Victorian.

A GHO ON THE GO

What would you say to a nationwide dress code? Bhutan has one.

The Kingdom of Bhutan is a small country bordered by China on one side and India on the other. In the shadow of these global powerhouses, Bhutan takes its identity very seriously—in 1989 a nationwide dress code forced all citizens to wear traditional costumes. Every man had to wear a knee-length coat called a *gho*, and **every woman had to wear a full-length dress called a *kira* and a jacket called a *tego* (right).** Color, fabric, and jewelry are determined by the person's status.

The dress code still exists, but it's more relaxed today. People are required to wear the national dress in government offices, at schools, and on special occasions. Otherwise, people can wear what they like—although many continue to opt for the traditional dress.

TIP OF THE HAT

The Aymara people live in the Andes and the Andean Plateau, in Bolivia, Peru, and Chile. Their ancestors also lived there for thousands of years, even before the Inca. Aymara men are known for their headwear, called *lluch'u*—colorful knitted caps with earflaps and pointy tops (bottom). Aymara women are famous for their **bowler hats** (inset). The story goes that a shipment of hats was originally sent over for English colonists in the 1800s, but the hats were too small. So the English gave the hats to local women. **Supposedly, a rumor circulated that wearing the hats cured infertility, and that's what led to their popularity.**

They are still worn a bit on the small side, perched on the woman's head at a jaunty angle and held in place with pins.

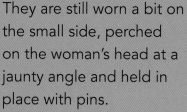

FOOTED FACTS

LOTUS shoes are beautifully embroidered shoes from China. But as lovely as they are, they can only be worn by women whose feet have been bound, a painful and crippling process.

TRIVAL boots from Mexico have very exaggerated, pointy ends. Some of the boots extend upward for several feet and turn into snake heads, disco balls, or other shapes.

AHENEMA are sandals from Ghana. Traditionally made from wood and other plant materials, ahenema were originally worn only by chiefs and other prominent people.

GETA (below) are Japanese sandals that are traditionally worn with kimonos. They have a strap that fits between the toes and wood bottoms that are a few inches thick, to keep the wearer's feet safely off the ground.

KLOMPEN are wooden clogs from the Netherlands. The oldest pair in existence was made in the mid-13th century.

Time Is on Our Side

The time and the date are pretty much the same for everybody, right? Not even close!

HAVE YOU GOT THE TIME?

China is the fourth-largest country in the world, and yet **it only has one time zone**. How can it possibly be 8 p.m. in Kashgar, on China's western border with Afghanistan, and also be 8 p.m. in Shanghai, more than 3,000 miles (5,000 km) away on the East China Sea? Basically, the reason is that nobody gets to tell the Chinese government what time it is.

Beginning in 1912, China was divided into five time zones. But after the revolution in 1949, the People's Republic of China announced that only one time zone would be observed throughout the country. Interestingly, although **the time zone is called "Beijing Time," the time actually has nothing to do with Beijing** (above). The official time in China is based on Shaanxi Province, in the geographical center of the country. People in the rest of the country have simply learned to adjust the hours they work, eat, and sleep to fit that time.

SUN AND MOON

The most-used calendar in the world is the Gregorian calendar. Introduced by Pope Gregory VIII in 1582, the Gregorian calendar is **solar**, meaning that **the number of days is based on the Earth's revolution around the sun**. The Gregorian calendar replaced Julius Caesar's Julian calendar from 43 BCE. The Julian calendar was also solar but had gotten out of sync with the movements of the sun.

The Islamic calendar is **lunar**, meaning it's **based on the phases of the moon**. Although Islamic countries use the Gregorian calendar for nonreligious purposes, the Islamic calendar determines when Muslim holidays are observed (above). Similarly, the Buddhist and Hebrew calendars are **lunisolar**, meaning they take **both the moon and the sun into account**. Then there's Orthodox Christianity, which has stuck with the Julian calendar, and that's why Orthodox Easter is later than Catholic Easter.

YESTERDAY AND TOMORROW

The International Date Line is **a made-up line** that cuts through the Pacific Ocean and divides one day from the next. As Earth spins on its axis, the International Date Line is the place where Monday turns into Tuesday, and so on.

The islands of Samoa (right) sit right on the international dateline. Because of that, it was the last place on Earth to see the sunset each day. For a long time, their travel slogan was **"We're so relaxed, it's yesterday!"** But in 2011 an extraordinary thing happened. Samoan calendars jumped from December 29 to December 31. Yes, December 30, 2011, did not exist in Samoa. This time-travel was done to shift the country from one side of the International Date Line to the other. The leap was made to more closely align the Samoan calendar with Australia and New Zealand, who are Samoa's main trading partners.

Alas, this change meant that Samoa had to give up its claim to having the latest sunset of the day. However, things aren't so bad—Samoa now has Earth's *earliest* sunrise.

START MAKING SENSE

The names we use for months are, quite simply, bonkers. *Sept* is Latin for seven, *octo* in Latin means eight, *novem* is nine and *decem* is ten, and yet September is the ninth month, October is tenth, November is eleventh, and December is twelfth! What's going on?

Here's the story. The original Roman calendar had ten months. **A new year kicked off with March, named for Mars, the god of war.** (At the time, people believed the beginning of the year was the right time to kick off a new war.) Emperor Numa Pompilius (753 to 673 BCE) added two months to the calendar. January, named for Janus, the god of doorways, was put at the beginning. February was added on to the end of the year, and only later moved to the second month.

Pompilius created a third month, Mercedonius (work month), as sort of a "leap month" that would happen some years but not others. Mercedonius could be added to the calendar at the whim of Rome's top religious leader. Julius Caesar (left) canceled Mercedonius in 43 BCE, when he replaced the old Roman calendar with a shiny new one named, naturally, after himself.

LIFE STAGES

Within a lifetime we all follow the same general steps in human development. **We are born, we are children, we make the transition into adulthood, we gradually age** (hopefully we stick around for a good long time), and then eventually we die. ALL CULTURES HAVE DIFFERENT WAYS OF MARKING AND CELEBRATING THESE STAGES.

The Wodaabe people of western Africa (right) have an annual **wife-stealing festival** (called Guérewol) that's pretty much what it sounds like. Men wear traditional dress and try to impress one another's wives.

The Greek island of **IKARIA** (below) is often referred to as "the island where people forget to die." That's only a bit of an exaggeration— **about one-third of the residents are 90 or older.**

IKARIA ISL.

Agios Polykarpos
Evdilos Karavostamo
Glaredos
Arethousa
Vrakades Christos
Hrysostomos Xyl
Manganitis

For **VALENTINE'S DAY** in Japan, women give sweets and gifts to the men in their lives, instead of the other way around.

Hello, World
In every culture, the arrival of a new baby is cause for celebration, community, and serious sleep deprivation.

COULD I HAVE . . . *TWO* BLANKETS?

In some countries, it is extremely common for parents to put their babies and young children outside to nap—not just at certain times of the year, but all year round. Can you guess what countries those are? Somewhere in the Caribbean, right?

Try Iceland, Finland, Sweden, and Norway. Nordic parents believe in spending as much time outside as possible, regardless of the weather. That includes napping outside even when the snow drifts are high. Parents claim children are healthier and sleep better that way.

But don't worry! As a woman in Stockholm told a reporter, "When the temperature drops to 5 degrees Fahrenheit (-15°C), we always cover the [strollers] with blankets." *Tak, Mamma!* (Thanks, Mom!)

CATCH ME IF YOU CAN

Worshipers at the Baba Umer Dargah shrine in Solapur, India, take part in a tradition that dates back some 700 years—**throwing their babies off the roof**.

According to legend, the practice began back at a time when infant mortality rates were extremely high. Desperate parents went to the shrine to beg for help for their sick children, and they were told to demonstrate their faith by dropping their babies off the roof. When the parents did so, a miraculous hammock appeared in mid-air and brought the babies (now healthy) safely down to the ground.

Although baby tossing is strongly discouraged by the government, it does still occur. These days, however, a group of men stand ready to catch the babies, just in case the magic hammock doesn't arrive.

I'VE BEEN HERE BEFORE

In Bali (right), traditional culture considers newborns to be divine vessels for the reincarnated souls of their ancestors. Consequently, **babies must be constantly carried and can't be allowed to touch the ground for the first three months of their lives.** After three months, a ceremony called Tigang Odalan is held, and the baby is placed on the ground for the first time. This marks the baby's "return to Earth." Babies are also given names in this ceremony.

TROUBLE WITH TWO

Some African tribes believe that giving birth to twins is a bad omen, particularly if the twins are the couple's first children. In Chinua Achebe's classic novel, *Things Fall Apart*, it's mentioned that the Igbo people viewed twins as "an offence on the land," and therefore the babies had to be left in the forest to die, to appease "the great goddess." Among indigenous people in what's now the country of Eritrea, twins aren't necessarily murdered, but they and their mothers may be forced out of their village.

Meanwhile, many other African tribes take the opposite view of twins. The Luo, Kalenjin, and Meru communities all consider twins to be a **great blessing** and the mothers who birth them to be **heroic**. And according to the religion of the Yoruba people, twins are born under the protection of Shango, the god of thunder and lightning, and they may possess supernatural powers.

THE DEVIL'S JUMP

Every June, the Spanish village of Castrillo de Murcia celebrates a festival called **El Colacho**. Men dressed as devils (right) run in the streets before being defeated and cast out. While you might go to Castrillo de Murica for the devils, you stay for the baby jumping.

All the babies born in the previous 12 months are lined up on pillows and put in the middle of the streets. The costumed devils then leap over the babies—an act that transfers the sins of the babies over to the devils. **After *el salto del colacho* (the devil's jump), the babies are showered with rose petals and returned to their parents.** Thus far, no baby-jumping-related injuries have been reported.

Growing Up

This might sound strange, but "childhood" is a concept that had to be invented. Even today, every culture views childhood a bit differently.

VISITORS FROM ANOTHER WORLD

Many cultures assume that kids don't know anything about anything until adults teach them. But a small ethnic group called the Beng, who live in Western Africa, completely reverse that relationship.

Beng children are believed to be the reincarnations of deceased relatives. They return to Earth from a spirit world called Wrugbe, where everything is known about everything. Young children are thought to understand every language due to their connection to that other world. In fact, it's said that spirits are pretty reluctant to leave *Wrugbe* at all; Beng parents must be very kind to their children, in order to convince them to stay.

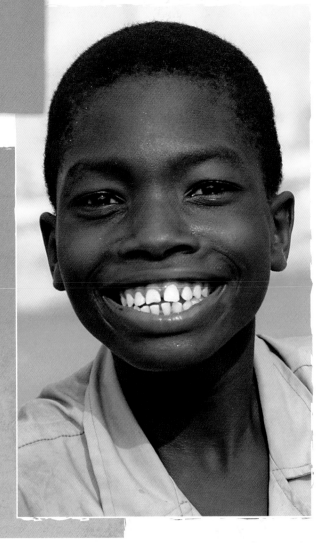

I CAN DO IT MYSELF

Little kids can often be heard boldly declaring that they can do this or that thing "all by myself." But when it comes to the Fulani (or Fulɓe) people in western and central Africa, this is quite true—certainly when it comes to Fulani girls. **Toddler girls carry dolls on their backs, in preparation for soon carrying their younger siblings**. By age four, girls are expected to be able to take care of their sisters and brothers and also do basic chores like fetching firewood. Two years later, the girls are making butter, pounding grain, and helping their moms sell goods at market.

SO IT IS WRITTEN

Children in North Korea must be registered with three agencies: at the town hall (makes sense), with the police (okaaayy), and also with the secret police (yikes!).

Stamped on every child's paperwork is his or her *songbun*. **A *songbun* is a person's social class; it is determined at birth and cannot be changed.** There are five official classes in North Korea: special, nucleus, basic, complex, and (by far the worst) hostile. A person's *songbun* is based on two factors, both relating to the father: one is the father's social status, and the other is his ancestry—specifically, the role the father's family played in the Korean War. The more helpful the ancestors were in the war effort, the better the *songbun*.

A *songbun* determines the course of a child's life. That includes what schools he or she can attend, what jobs he or she can have, and even where he or she can live. People with poor *songbuns* are not allowed to live in the capital city of Pyongyang.

ONE SIZE DOES NOT FIT ALL

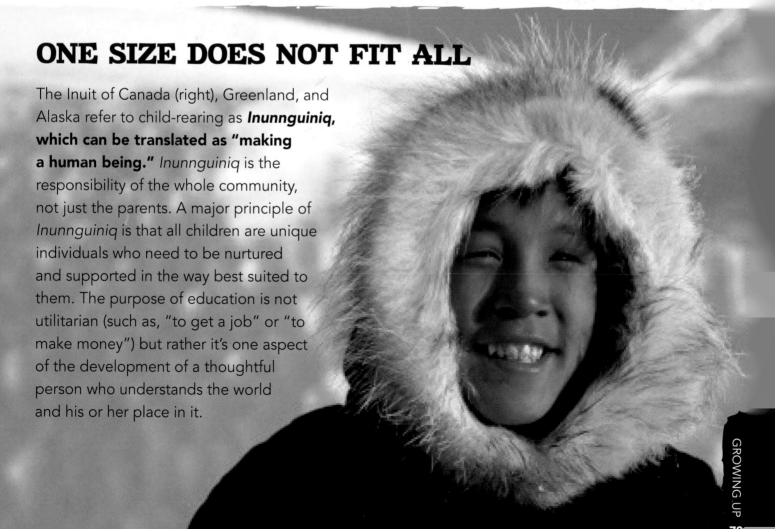

The Inuit of Canada (right), Greenland, and Alaska refer to child-rearing as ***Inunnguiniq,*** **which can be translated as "making a human being."** *Inunnguiniq* is the responsibility of the whole community, not just the parents. A major principle of *Inunnguiniq* is that all children are unique individuals who need to be nurtured and supported in the way best suited to them. The purpose of education is not utilitarian (such as, "to get a job" or "to make money") but rather it's one aspect of the development of a thoughtful person who understands the world and his or her place in it.

Almost Adults

There are about 1.2 billion teens and preteens in the world. Half of them live in Asia, and nearly 90 percent live in developing countries, where life might be a lot different from where you are.

STATE OF THE TEENS

UNICEF, which is the United Nations organization focused on the welfare of children and teens, regularly publishes data about teenagers around the world. Here are just a few statistics they uncovered.

- Adolescents make up about **18 percent of the overall world population**.
- An estimated 127 million people between the ages of 15 and 24 are not able to read or write.
- Injuries are the leading cause of death among the world's teenagers. "Injuries" include traffic accidents, falls, and drowning, as well as violence.
- About 2.2 million teenagers are living with HIV/AIDS; about 60 percent are female.
- In South Asia, almost one-third of girls aged 15 to 19 are already married.
- About 50,000 girls under the age of 19 die in childbirth every year.
- About one in five teens in the world experiences some sort of mental health issue, such as major depression or anxiety.

MY RUSSIAN ROMANCE

Ever since the first Stone Age mom said, **"You can't leave the cave looking like that,"** adults have been fretting about teenagers and their fashion choices. But leave it to Vladimir Putin's Russia to turn black lipstick into a national emergency.

   Beginning in 2007–2008, hardline Russian politicians began pushing for a ban on so-called emo music and fashion, such as **black clothing, pink hair, facial piercings, and studded belts**. They argued that emo encourages suicide, and that a ban was necessary to "curb dangerous teen trends." The legislation, entitled "Government Strategy in the Sphere of Spiritual and Ethical Education," has thus far not been signed into law.

ADULTHOOD THE HARD WAY

Maybe you think that learning Hebrew for your bar mitzvah or practicing dance steps for your quinceañera sounds tough, but teens in Western countries have no idea how easy they have it when it comes to the transition into adulthood.

- Among the Hamar tribe in Ethiopia (below), a boy becomes a man in a ceremony called *bullah* (bull jumping), in which he demonstrates **he can run across the backs of a line of bulls without falling**. Also, both young men and women must accept a scar-inducing whipping from their elders, to demonstrate their devotion to the tribe.

- When girls become women on the Mentawai Islands in Indonesia, they have their **teeth sharpened into points**. Very sharp teeth are considered beautiful in Mentawai culture. The process is done with chisels and no anesthetic.

- Papua New Guinea's Chambri tribe practices a scarification ritual in which boys are cut with razor blades. The patterns are designed such that, when they heal, their skin will resemble the skins of crocodiles living in the Sepik River. The process is said to be unbelievably painful, but the pain is the point—the Chambri believe that the ability to withstand extreme pain is a necessary part of adulthood.

Memorizing a bit of the Torah doesn't seem so bad now, does it?

Thank You for Being a Friend

When it comes to relationships, romance gets most of the attention. But the truth is, we can't get by without our friends.

TAKE THE DAY

Many countries set aside days for the celebration of friendship. Friendship Day was allegedly invented in 1930 by businessman and Hallmark card company founder J. C. Hall. Despite its obvious commercial motivation, Friendship Day is celebrated in many countries—but it falls on different days, depending on where you are.

South American countries get particularly excited about their versions of Friendship Day. Arguably, some of them may get too excited—on July 20, 2005, a flood of "Friend's Day" phone calls were blamed for a shutdown of the cell phone network in Buenos Aires and a number of other Argentine cities.

In Colombia, Dia de Amor y Amistad (Love and Friendship Day) is September 15. In keeping with the commercial spirit of the original Friendship Day, Colombians apparently chose September 15 because the country has no other holidays in September.

Paraguay has a Friendship Day ritual similar to "Secret Santa," except it's called Amigo Invisible (Invisible Friend). Names are distributed among friends who give small gifts to each other on July 30.

МОИ ДРУЗЬЯ (MY FRIENDS)

Russians take friendship very seriously—one way you can tell is by the number of proverbs they have about the significance of friends. Here are just a few:

- Better to have 100 friends than 100 rubles.
- Walking in the darkness with a friend is better than walking alone in the light.
- One old friend is better than two new ones.
- Old friends and old wine are best.
- A friend to all is a friend to none.

GREETINGS, FRIEND

In the Arab world, male friends holding hands is considered normal—it's common in Algeria, Kuwait, Saudi Arabia, the United Arab Emirates, and other countries. Male friends also hold hands in many African countries, such as Namibia, Rwanda, and Zambia. It's just not a big deal.

THE WRONG GIFTS TO GIVE IN CHINA

If you want to give a gift to a friend from China, do a little research first. Particular gifts have strong associations and could be taken the wrong way.

A KNIFE or pair of scissors (above) may be interpreted as you wanting to "sever" your friendship. (This belief exists in a surprising number of countries, from Bosnia to Mozambique to Ukraine! Maybe just stay away from sharp gifts, to be safe.)

A BLANKET suggests you think your friend is going to be broke very soon.

A CLOCK suggests you are anticipating your friend's death. The reason is that the word for *clock* in Chinese is pronounced "song-zhong," which sounds too close to the word for death in some dialects. (Giving your friend a watch, however, is just fine!)

Will You Be Mine?

Marriage has changed a lot since the first recorded nuptials took place in Mesopotamia in 2350 BCE. It would take another 4,000 years, into Europe's Middle Ages, for the sound of wedding bells to finally mean that two people had found true love.

IMAGINE THE THANK-YOU NOTES . . .

The record for the largest wedding reception is held by Indian film star and chief of the Tamil Nadu, Jayaram Jayalalithaa. Although she was the host of the festivities in 1995, she wasn't the bride: the wedding was held in Madras (now Chennai), India, for her foster son and his new wife. **There were 150,000 guests!**

LOOKING FOR LOVE IN IRISH PLACES

Most of the year, the tiny Irish town of Lisdoonvarna in County Clare has fewer than 800 residents. But come September, lonely hearts flock by the thousands to the town's annual Matchmaking Festival (below). **Professional matchmaker Willy Day claims to have brought together more than 3,000 successful couples.** He explained to a reporter that the process is very simple. Someone seeking a mate should simply go to his office (which is a bar, by the way), fill out a brief form, and before you know it, Willy will have someone in mind who is perfect for you.

DON'T FEEL OBLIGATED

Although originally a Western holiday, Valentine's Day officially arrived in Japan in 1936. That's when the Morozoff Company—a Japanese candy company founded by a Russian immigrant—bought the country's first Valentine's Day advertisement. But in Japan, women give sweets and gifts to the men in their lives, instead of the other way around (below). Deciding which gentlemen should get which gift is a complex process. **If she loves you, you get *honmei choko* (true feeling chocolate)**, but if she doesn't have feelings for you, you get ***giri choko* (obligation chocolate)**.

COURTSHIP FACTS

Social mores evolve over time—a good thing because some of the old-time courtship rituals were . . . well, they weren't great.

IN THE AUSTRIAN FARMLANDS of the 1800s, a young Austrian farm gal would go to a dance with sliced apples under her armpits. If she danced with an intriguing young man, she'd give him one of the apple slices to eat, so the young man could smell her.

THE ATAYAL are an indigenous people of Taiwan. Traditionally, before young Atayal men were allowed to marry, they had to **kill an enemy and bring his severed head back** to the village for display.

IN VIKING SOCIETY, it was a big mistake for a young man to write love poems or songs for the woman he was courting. Writing such things implied that he knew her a little too well. The father and brothers of the bride-to-be were well within their rights to **kill poetry-writing suitors**.

Getting Older

In the words of the famously suave French actor Maurice Chevalier: "Old age isn't so bad when you consider the alternative."

TÉLÉPHONEZ À VOTRE MAMAN!

Article 207 of France's civil code requires people to stay in touch with their aging parents. The law was passed in 2004 after the country was gripped by a heat wave that killed about 15,000 people—most were old folks who'd been left alone while their ungrateful children were away on summer vacation. Under the law, nonphoners can be punished with fines or even jail time.

A MYTH OF SACRIFICE

You may have heard that Inuit people put their elderly on ice floes and send them off to die. This is *almost* entirely a myth. It's true that there were certain moments when the Inuit experienced severe famine; with resources dwindling, decisions had to be made about who could be kept alive. In that context, old people were sometimes abandoned. But that was a response to a catastrophic, life-or-death situation—it was not some beloved cultural practice. **This myth was likely spread by a film called *The Savage Innocents* (1960) starring Anthony Quinn.**

THAT DEPENDS

Japan has more than 67,000 people aged 100 or older (centenarians). It's the highest rate of centenarians in the world. Not only does Japan have a large elderly population, the country has a low birth rate. For that reason, Japan has been described as a **"demographic time bomb."** More adult diapers are bought in Japan every year than baby diapers.

FORGETFUL ISLAND?

The Greek island of Ikaria (right) is often referred to as **"the island where people forget to die."** That's only a bit of an exaggeration—about one-third of the residents are 90 or older. Ikaria residents are frequently interviewed by reporters trying to understand the secret of long life. In the opinion of Ioanna Proiou, 105, what you eat is less important than how you spend your time. She advised a reporter, "Do something that stirs your passion."

THE ANCIENT ANCIENTS

There's a common misconception that a 40-year-old person would have been considered "ancient" in ancient Rome (below). People think this because the average life span in ancient Rome has been calculated to have been about 35 years. Therefore, the thinking goes, truly old people must have been as rare as four-leaf clovers.

But that misunderstands how an average is calculated. Infant mortality rates were much higher than they are today, as were deaths in childhood. **One study suggested that babies in ancient Rome had only a 50–50 chance of reaching their tenth birthday.** All that early death drags down the average life span quite a bit! For Romans who made it past childhood, their survival prospects got better. In fact, "old age" has been defined as beginning at around 60 or 65 years old since the first century BCE.

Final Passage

How people in different countries respond to death can tell us their beliefs about life.

TURN THE BONES

Famadihana (turning of the bones) is a tradition in Madagascar (right). Once every five (or sometimes seven) years, **Malagasy people go to their graveyards, dig up the bodies of their deceased family members, and spray them with either wine or perfume.** *Famadihana* is an important family and community event, where there is music and dancing (sometimes with the bodies).

BREAKING THE VESSEL

In the rocky landscape of Tibet, burying the dead underground is often impossible. Instead, some Tibetans hold "sky funerals" (below) for their deceased loved ones. In a sky funeral, the person's corpse is prepared and laid outside to be consumed by vultures.

Buddhism teaches that life is impermanent. **Death just means the person's spirit has moved out of their physical vessel and on to the next part of its journey.** So, while a sky funeral might sound weird to you, viewed from a Buddhist perspective it can be beautiful. The custom allows the "vessel" that is the human body to release the soul within and metaphorically take to the sky. Although sky funerals are most associated with Tibet, they are sometimes done in Bhutan and Mongolia as well.

GOING OUT IN STYLE

Ghana is well known for its **"fantasy coffins" (right).** Designed and built specifically for the person who has passed, they are meant to reflect something about that person's life or career. Why be buried in an old pine box when you can travel to the next world in a giant fish (for a fisherman), **a giant ear of corn** (for a farmer), or a giant wrench (for a mechanic)?

CITY OF THE DEAD

About half of New Orleans sits below sea level, which means anything buried is likely to pop back up again. As a result, **many cemeteries had to be built above ground**. The stone crypts and mausoleums are arranged in street-like patterns, which resulted in the city's graveyards being nicknamed "Cities of the Dead."

Another important part of death in New Orleans is the jazz funeral (below). Traditionally, sad music is played as the mourners walk to the burial, and then afterwards, joyful music is played as the mourners head home. **The shift from sad music to happy signifies that, while we do mourn the loss of our loved ones, we also know that life must continue.** It's also important to know that the tradition began among New Orleans's African slaves. Death, while tragic, also granted a release from the bonds of slavery and into the joy of eternal life.

RELIGION AND FAITH

Today there are **several thousand different religions.**
Giving an exact number is impossible, because it depends on how you
define the word "religion." But there are twelve that are considered the
"classical world religions," and then there are thousands of smaller faiths,
including indigenous religions.

Somewhere between 10 and 15 percent of the population of Egypt are Coptic Christians. This branch of Christianity traces its roots back to Saint Mark, who brought Christianity to Alexandria in roughly 42 CE.

Among the more unusual religions are groups of people who worship **UFOs**, **STAR WARS** characters, and even the soccer player **DIEGO MARADONA**.

World Religions

World religions have large numbers of followers—they unite people across many different communities and countries.

SPIRITUAL PROJECTIONS

Christianity is currently the world's largest religion—with around 2.2 billion Christians, that's about a third of the world's population. Coming in second is **Islam (right), with 1.6 billion followers**, and the third-largest religious affiliation is none at all, with **1.1 billion atheists and agnostics**.

Projections suggest that Islam is catching up to Christianity. If current trends continue, there will be roughly the same number of Muslims as Christians by 2050. Muslims have the highest birthrates, averaging 3.1 children per family, as compared to 2.7 per Christian family. The ranks of the unaffiliated will also increase, but not as quickly; atheists have an average of 1.7 children per family—the lowest rate of any religion except Buddhists.

NEWCOMERS

The Baha'i faith (below) is the youngest of the "big twelve" world religions. It was founded in what's now Iran in the 1860s. An offshoot of Islam, people of the **Baha'i faith believe that all religions are legitimate because they all worship different versions of the same God.** Their symbol is the nine-pointed star, which is meant to represent the unity of all different faiths. Baha'i believers are essentially pacifists, but their faith does allow for self-defense. The Baha'i faith isn't recognized as legitimate by the Iranian government; nevertheless, there are in the neighborhood of 8 million Baha'i followers all over the world.

I SPY WITH MY THIRD EYE

Unlike many world religions, Hinduism does not have one specific founder or prophet. It evolved gradually in the Indus Valley around 2300 BCE. Hindus believe in the idea of one God, called Brahman, who can take many different forms or incarnations. The "big three" are **Brahma, the creator of the universe, Vishnu, the preserver, and Shiva, the destroyer and transformer.**

It might sound strange to worship a god devoted to destruction, but Hindus believe that without destruction there can be no creation, so the two forces go hand in hand. Shiva is famous for having a third eye in the center of his forehead, which is sometimes associated with lofty spiritual wisdom. That's not all, though—in some Hindu mythology, **Shiva can use his third eye to destroy his enemies; he simply looks at them and burns them to cinders.** Don't get on Shiva's bad side.

THE HOUSE OF ISRAEL

Ethiopia is a country with deep religious roots. Not only was it an early adopter of Christianity but Ethiopia also has a long-standing Jewish population, who are called **Beta Israel** (House of Israel).

There are a lot of theories! Some say the Ethiopian Jews are descendants of the legendary Ethiopian king Menelik I, himself the son of King Solomon and the Queen of Sheba. Others argue that the ancestors of today's Ethiopian Jews arrived as refugees after Egypt

conquered Judah in 568 BCE. Yet another theory claims that Beta Israel actually started out as Christians but came to identify themselves as Jewish over time.

FAITH FACTS

IN 1910, TWO-THIRDS OF THE WORLD'S CHRISTIANS LIVED IN EUROPE. One hundred years later, only one-third of all Christians were European. Today, Nigeria has twice as many Christians as Germany does.

MOSQUES IN TAJIKISTAN often have a painting of a horse's hoofprint. The hoofprint reminds worshippers of the legendary journey of an imam (religious leader) and the son-in-law of Muhammad, Ali ibn Abi Talib, who once rode across the region, punishing unbelievers.

IT'S A MYTH THAT ALL HINDUS ARE VEGETARIAN— many are, but not all—or that they "worship" cows. But they do believe that cows are sacred and should be honored, which is why the majority of Hindus won't eat them.

Traditional Beliefs

Beyond the dominant faiths, there's a whole lot to know about indigenous people and their religions.

THE PEACOCK ANGEL

The Yazīdī (right) are a Kurdish ethnic group who live mainly in the northern parts of Iraq but also in northern Syria, southern Turkey, and parts of Iran. They practice their own ancient religion, **Yazīdīsm**, which blends aspects of Zoroastrianism with Judaism, Islam, and Christianity.

According to Yazīdīsm, **the world was created by a supreme God who then left it in the hands of seven divine beings**—the chief one is Malak Ṭāʾūs (Peacock Angel). Malak Ṭāʾūs has been misrepresented as being analogous to Satan because, like Satan, he is a "fallen angel." However, Malak Ṭāʾūs was forgiven by God and is not at all evil. Unfortunately, this error has dire consequences for the world's 700,000 Yazīdī. The Islamic State (ISIS), an extremist offshoot of the terrorist group al Qaeda, has targeted the Yazīdī for genocide because they're wrongly believed to be Satanists.

YES, WE CANDOMBLÉ

Candomblé is a religion that evolved in the 19th century and today is practiced mainly in Brazil but also in other parts of South America. It blends the beliefs of West African slaves and indigenous peoples of the region, borrowing some elements from Catholicism, too. **Candomblé gods, called *orixás*, determine the fate of human beings.** The top deity is Olodumare, who communicates with humans by way of the god-messenger Exu. In addition to being the name of the faith, **candomblé is also the name of an all-night dance** (right) that worshippers perform to honor the *orixás*.

DREAMTIME

The original Australians, called aboriginal people, migrated there from Africa about 65,000 years ago. Today, they make up about 2 percent of Australia's population. Many aboriginal Australians (right) continue their traditional spiritual practices, but they can be hard for outsiders to understand; the English language doesn't have useful words to even describe them. The most commonly used term is **"Dreamtime,"** a reference to the beginning of everything, **when the Spirits and the Ancestors created the world**.

VOODOO IN OUIDAH

The West African country of Benin is the birthplace of the folk religion called Voodoo (left). Ouidah, on the coast of Benin, was once a center of the 19th-century African slave trade, and **it's now the heart of the Voodoo tradition**. About 10,000 Voodoo practitioners travel to Ouidah every year for their annual festival. The highlight of the festival is a ceremony at the Door of No Return, which marks the spot where ancestors were forced onto slave ships to cross the Atlantic. (There were four **Doors of No Return**—in addition to the one in Benin, the most infamous is on Gorée, an island off Senegal, and the other two are in Ghana and Gambia.)

DON'T DO THAT!

The word **"taboo,"** for something forbidden, comes to us from Polynesian religions. The explorer James Cook heard the word while traveling in Tonga (below) in the 18th century, and he introduced it to English-speakers back home.

Keepers of the Faith

For a religion to survive, it has to be lovingly maintained, with beliefs and traditions passed along from generation to generation.

SEND MORE EGGS!

Mount Athos (right) is an autonomous monastic state in Greece. "Holy Mountain," as it is known, has been an important site to the Greek Orthodox Church since 1054. It is home to some 20 monasteries that house about 1,400 monks. **Women and children are not allowed**, not even for brief visits. **Even female animals aren't permitted on Mount Athos**. The monks have to have eggs brought up the mountain for them, because they aren't allowed to keep hens. But cats are allowed because ... the monasteries have a bit of a mouse problem.

THE CARETAKERS

The Church of the Holy Sepulchre in Jerusalem (below) contains both the site of Christ's crucifixion and Christ's empty tomb. **The caretaker of the church is a Palestinian Muslim named Adeeb Joudeh Al Husseini.** The caretaker job goes way back in his family—and I mean, way back. Members of his family have looked after one of Christianity's holiest places since the 12th century.

Meanwhile in Kolkata, India, Muslims look after three local synagogues. When India was a British colony, Kolkata was home to about 3,000 Jews, but that number has decreased to a few dozen. Still, Nasser Sheikh has been looking after one of the synagogues for over 50 years, and his son Osim will carry on after he's gone. Sheikh says it is not so strange that Muslims should care for the holy sites of other faiths. "The Koran, the Torah, and the Bible have similar origins," he told a reporter. "How then could we be fighting?"

SIXTY-YEAR SIGUI

The Sigui Festival is a once-in-a-generation religious ritual among the Dogon people of Mali (right and below left); the goal of the ceremony is to pass on spiritual knowledge from one generation to the next. The festival is held only once every 60 or so years—the precise date is determined by the position of the star Sirius. **Participants carve masks and dance in procession from village to village**, and there is a secret language for participants to learn, which can take years. The last Sigui Festival was held in the late 1960s, and estimates vary as to when the next one will begin—some sources say 2027, others 2032.

THE CUT-AND-PASTE BIBLE

In 1820, America's "founding father" and former president Thomas Jefferson sat down with a copy of the King James Bible, some paste, and a razor blade. With these crude tools, **he created his own version of the Bible by cutting and pasting the parts he liked and getting rid of the rest.** *The Life and Morals of Jesus of Nazareth* keeps the parts about morality but gets rid of Christ's miracles, his resurrection, and anything supernatural like angels or descriptions of Heaven and Hell. Now called "the Jefferson Bible," the original (left) is held in the Smithsonian (and can be read online, should you want to see it). To be fair, Jefferson himself never called his work a Bible—it was just a personal project for himself.

New Arrivals

All old religions were new at some point. Will any of these more recent spiritual inventions have staying power?

JOIN OUR CULT, YOU WILL

A religion that blends beliefs and practices from other religions is referred to as **syncretic**. Japan's Happy Science Church has got to be one of the oddest syncretic religions around. Founded by

businessman Ryuho Okawa in 1986, Happy Science blends beliefs from Christianity, Buddhism, and . . . um . . . the Star Wars universe. Okawa claims that he is the reincarnation of great spiritual leaders like **Buddha, Jesus Christ, and, of course, Yoda (left)**. But according to one writer who attended Happy Science training, Okawa has only bad things to say about both Chinese and Korean people—doesn't seem very Yoda-like, now does it?

CARGO, COME BACK

In the 1940s, South Pacific islanders (right) found themselves smack in the middle of World War II. Exposed to the modern world for the first time, **many islanders thought the apocalypse had come.**

Both Japan and the United States shipped massive amounts of goods to the soldiers fighting in and around islands like Vanuatu, Fiji, and New Guinea. Natives were stunned by it all—clothes, processed foods, weapons. They'd never seen anything like that before, and once the war ended, they stopped seeing it entirely. So-called **cargo cults** sprang up across the islands, in which people came to believe that a messiah would come, bringing the riches of the Europeans back with him. Some cargo cults even built bamboo versions of airplanes, landing strips, and docks, in hopes of coaxing the goods to return.

HALLOWED BE THY FOOT

Iglesia Maradoniana is an extremely specialized church in Argentina that worships the soccer star Diego Maradona, who is considered by church followers to be the greatest player of all time.

At the 1986 World Cup final against Great Britain, Maradona famously scored a goal that might—depending on whom you ask—have involved him punching the ball into the net. Maradona claimed it was not his hand but the "Hand of God" that directed the ball and brought victory to Argentina. Either way, the Iglesia Maradoniana has thousands of followers, both in Argentina and around the world. Followers have even developed their own version of the Ten Commandments, such as **"Love football above all else."**

I WANT TO BELIEVE

Mix some yoga, a teaspoon of Hinduism, a pinch of Buddhism, and a half a cup of space aliens, and what do you get? You get the Aetherius Society, which was founded in 1954 by Englishman George King. Members of the Aetherius Society believe that humanity's worst problems can be solved if we follow the path to enlightenment set out by the **"Gods from space."** The aliens, called Cosmic Masters, want to aid human progress but are thwarted by dark governmental forces known as the Silence Group. King died (or moved on?) in 1997, but the Aetherius Society continues. It still has followers in England, Ghana, Japan, New Zealand, Nigeria, and the Los Angeles area of California.

Keep the Day Holy

Every religion has its special days, where daily life stops and believers reflect on what makes their faith special.

LIGHT UP THE NIGHT

For people of Hindu faith, the biggest holiday is Diwali, or the Festival of Lights (right), which takes place in the fall. It celebrates the triumph of light over darkness and, by extension, of good over evil. Diwali, which is also observed by some Buddhists, Jains, and Sikhs, typically lasts five days. Sweet treats are the order of the day, such as dried fruit, fudge, laddu (Indian doughnut holes), and gujiyas (fruit-filled dumplings). Fireworks are an important part of Diwali celebrations—although recently there have been complaints that all the fireworks hurt the already-poor air quality in larger Indian cities.

HE, TOO, KNOWS WHEN YOU ARE SLEEPING

In Austria and parts of Germany, **Santa Claus has a dark side, and his name is Krampus** (below). A tall, demonic-looking creature with horns and hooves, Krampus arrives every December 5 (Krampusnacht) to punish naughty children with his big stick. To celebrate this grim version of the Christmas Spirit, some towns hold a Krampuslauf, in which groups of young Krampuses (Krampi?) run through the streets, whacking bystanders on the legs with their sticks.

THE SWEETEST EID

After a month of daytime fasting during Ramadan, Muslims all over the world are ready for some fun, which arrives in the form of **a three-day holiday called Eid al-Fitr** (Feast of the Fast-Breaking). Large, elaborate meals are shared among family, neighbors, and friends. Sometimes Eid al-Fitr is referred to as "Sweet Eid" because of all the desserts and sweet treats that are made. Gifts are given to children, and some shopkeepers give out Eid gifts to customers. The correct greeting to everyone you see during the holiday is "Eid Mubarak," which means "Blessed Eid."

LET THE GOOD TIMES ROLL

Where Catholic faith has traveled, you'll find a Carnival tradition. The word "carnival" comes from the Latin for "remove meat." This is because Carnival comes right before the religious observation of Lent, where traditionally people would abstain from meat to show their devotion. (These days, people can choose to give up other things to honor Lent—it doesn't have to be meat.) Since Lent is associated with self-denial, the period leading up to Lent is associated with excess—food, drink, music, dancing, or all of the above. The Italian city of **Venice is Europe's most famous Carnival-celebrating city, beloved for the intricate masks worn at Carnival celebrations**. Meanwhile, the entire country of Brazil is Carnival-crazy for the week before Lent, with massive parades, block parties, and some very intense samba competitions (right). Other cities with massive Carnival events include Santa Cruz de Tenerife, Spain; Oruru, Bolivia; Port of Spain, Trinidad and Tobago; and of course, New Orleans, Louisiana.

Free to Believe?

Freedom of religion is widely accepted as a fundamental human right, but that doesn't mean it has been achieved everywhere.

EVIL BREATHING?

Members of the Chinese group called Falun Gong (literally, "law wheel practice") have been persecuted for about two decades. Falun Gong is not a religion, exactly—it's more of a "spiritual practice" centered on meditation and controlled breathing. It was invented by Li Hongzhi, also known as Master Li, in the early 1990s. **Members of Falun Gong (left) believe that enlightenment can be found by studying and following the writings of Master Li.** But their devotion to him is viewed as a serious threat by the Communist government. In response, Falun Gong has been banned in China, and thousands of followers have been sent to "re-education camps." The group is considered enemy number one on the government's list of China's 24 most "evil cults."

UNDERSTANDING THE PROBLEM

Every few years, the Pew Research Center undertakes a global study of **religious freedom**. They take into account factors such as government-imposed restrictions and incidents of harassment (or "social hostilities") to try to determine which countries are more or less free when it comes to religion. They also catalog which religion was targeted in which place. Here are some examples from the report:

- Jews (right) were found to be the most-targeted group in countries such as Belarus, Brazil, Peru, Serbia, and Switzerland.
- Muslims were the most-targeted group in countries that included Australia, Burma, Denmark, Italy, the Netherlands, and Portugal.
- Both Muslims and Jews experienced targeting in Poland, Solvakia, the United Kingdom, and the United States.

A MIXED HISTORY

India is roughly 80 percent Hindu, 13 percent Muslim, 2 percent Christian, and the remainder Buddhist, Jainist, Zoroastrian, or Jewish. The country has a mixed history when it comes to religious tolerance. On the one hand, religious freedom is written into the Indian constitution, and the holiday traditions of different faiths are observed and enjoyed by many. On the other, the country experienced shocking moments of violence between the Hindu and Muslim populations.

In fact, India is the shape it is because the part of the country with a Muslim majority was split off and named Pakistan in 1947. But even that separation didn't end interfaith violence. For example, in 1992 Hindu extremists demolished the Babri Masjid mosque in Ayodhya—an event that sparked widespread rioting and resulted in the deaths of about 2,000 people. As recently as 2002, anti-Muslim rioting in the state of Gujarat resulted in more than 1,000 dead and 2,500 people injured.

FRIENDLY FACTS

MANY MUSLIMS in the city of Mithi, Pakistan, have decided to no longer eat cows, in order to be respectful of their Hindu neighbors.

THE TRINITY UNITED CHURCH in Nova Scotia, Canada, is known as the "mosque within a church." Trinity rents space to a small group of Muslims in the community, so that they will have a place to worship, too.

In Cameroon, **CHRISTIAN AND MUSLIM** locals banded together after a terrorist group, Boko Haram, began launching attacks.

Superstitious Minds

Whether you "knock on wood" for luck, whistle past the graveyard, or avoid the number 13, most of us can't avoid the occasional offbeat belief.

A WRIT OF PROTECTION

Although it's less common today than in the past, some Egyptians still participate in the tradition of attaching written passages to clothing to bring good luck or protect the wearer from misfortune. The writing can be quotes from the Koran (right) or simply a name—for instance, the name of a particular prophet. **Egyptian children sometimes have little bits of writing attached to their caps to protect them from evil.**

CROCODILE ROCK

Not far from Banjul, capital of The Gambia, lies a shrine called Bakau Kachikally, better known as the Kachikally Crocodile Pool. **Between 80 and 100 Nile crocodiles (below) live in the water**, which some believe can cure infertility in women. Visitors to Bakau Kachikally are a mix of local women hoping to get pregnant and foreign tourists who just want to take **selfies with the surprisingly friendly crocs**. The crocodile keepers accept small gifts from visitors, but they don't officially charge anything, as it's believed making a profit off of the pool would destroy its healing power.

YOU LOOKING AT ME?

One legend common to many places—36 percent, if you believe folklorist John Roberts—is **the dreaded evil eye**.

References to a glance that holds a curse can be found in the Bible, the Koran, Hindu stories, and the writings of Shakespeare. People in Latin American countries refer to it as *mal de ojo*. Meanwhile, the Greek evil eye is called *mati*. A *mati* pendant, which consists of a blue circle with lighter blue, white, and black circles within it, is a popular item used to ward off the curse. In Turkmenistan, some people believe that offering too much praise can actually bring on the evil eye.

People in Chad believe that looking directly at another person or thing will bring bad luck. If enough people stare at a tree, for example, eventually the tree will die. That may just be a legend, but the belief has real-life impacts. In Chad, making direct eye contact with someone you don't know well can be interpreted as a threat.

FOLKLORE FACTS

IN MEDIEVAL EUROPE, churchgoers would touch wood that they believed came from Jesus's cross. That's where the superstition "knock on wood" came from.

PEOPLE IN BOTH HUNGARY AND RUSSIA believe that it's bad luck to sit at the corner of a table.

IN NORWAY, you shouldn't whistle at the sun, because doing so will make it rain.

RWANDAN men say that a woman who eats goat meat will turn into one—bearded and stubborn. Rwandan women say that goat meat is delicious and Rwandan men are just trying to avoid sharing it.

IN SYRIA, a terrible drought was supposedly caused by a yo-yo—as a result, yo-yos have been banned there since 1933.

FOOD AND DRINK

Today, cooking and eating aren't just a question of survival but of identity, community, and even religious faith. Cultural values and personal taste also have big roles to play in what and how we eat. A highly sought after delicacy in one culture may be a stomach-churning prospect in another.

The Piaroa tribe in Venezuela roasts **tarantulas over an open fire**, while Cambodians prefer their tarantulas fried.

In Mexico and in neighborhoods of Southern California, it's not that unusual to see tacos made with **intestines** (taco de *tripas*) or **tongue** (taco de *lengua*), **pig stomach** (taco de *buche*), **brain** (taco de *sesos*) or a combination of **eyes**, **cheek**, and **brain** (taco de *cabeza*).

We Are What We Eat

Whether it's a hamburger in America, a strong "cuppa" in England, or cheesy poutine in Canada, all cultures have certain foods that are central to their national identities.

NOODLES OF INDEPENDENCE

The dish most strongly associated with Thailand has to be pad Thai (below), a **peanuty noodle dish that's usually served with fried tofu** and a meat such as shrimp or chicken. Interestingly, although Thailand is a very old country, pad Thai is a fairly young dish.

Legend has it that pad Thai was invented in the kitchen of Thailand's first prime minister, Plaek Phibunsongkhram (known as Phibun). In 1938, the Thai monarchy had just been removed from power. **Phibun wanted to encourage Thai people to come together as a new, free nation**. Part of his unification campaign involved sending out food carts all over the country to introduce Thai citizens to a new, "patriotic" dish: rice noodles, Thai-style . . . or pad Thai.

COLD COOKED

Ceviche (right) is a deliciously fascinating feat of science: **raw seafood is "cooked" by placing it in lime or lemon juice**. The acid in the citrus causes a chemical reaction that, essentially, cooks the fish without the use of heat. (It's not literally cooked, however; the technical term for the process is denaturation.) **Ceviche is considered the national dish of Peru**, where it's said that the Moche people on the country's northwest coast invented the procedure some 2,000 years ago. They used tumbo, a type of passionfruit, to "cook" their fish—one expert has suggested that mixing lime with grapefruit would be the best way to approximate tumbo's flavor.

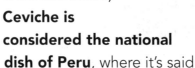

SAY WAT?

Ethiopian cuisine is famous the world over for not using plates. That's not strictly true, of course—there is one main plate in the center of the table, and **a large, sourdough flatbread called injera** (left) sits on top of it. Injera, which is made from a grain called teff, is soft and a bit spongy—imagine a pancake but not sweet. Stews such as doro wat (chicken) and sheir be kibbe (legumes) go on top of the injera, and then diners eat by tearing off pieces of the injera and scooping up the toppings.

HERDER'S MEAT

The national dish of Hungary is a beef stew called goulash (right). **The name comes from the inventors of the dish—the gulyás, horse-riding cattlemen of Central Europe.** Much like the cowboys of the American West, the gulyás did a lot of cooking in big pots that were set over an open flame. That cooking style gave rise to gulyás hús ("herder's meat") that we now know as goulash.

The stew became intertwined with Hungarian identity in the 19th century, when the region was ruled by the Habsburgs (German royalty). People increasingly wanted to embrace their own culture—called Magyar—rather than allow their traditions to be replaced by German ones. Serving herder's meat became a way of reinforcing connections to Magyar history.

Melting Pots

Fusion cuisine is the blending of two or more cuisines into a new and delectable third.

YOU SAY CHALAKILIS, I SAY CHILAQUILES

Guam is a US territory in the western Pacific, part of the Micronesian island chain. The largest group of indigenous Guamanians are the Chamorro. At various points, Guam has been colonized by the Spanish and Portuguese; the island is also home to Filipino, Korean, and Japanese people. Guanamanian food reflects the territory's complicated history.

For example, one popular dish is *daigo kimchi*, which blends Korean and Japanese influences. **Kimchi (right) is a traditional Korean dish of pickled cabbage**, but the Guanamanian version is made with daikon radish and cucumber and eaten as an appetizer. A popular meat dish in Guam is *chalakilis*, which is somewhat similar (both

in name and in recipe) to the Mexican dish called *chilaquiles*—except where *chilaquiles* uses tortilla strips, *chalakilis* uses rice.

KIWI ADAPTATIONS

The food of New Zealand blends indigenous Māori traditions with the influences of British colonists. For instance, many dishes that were made with white potatoes back in England are prepared with sweet potatoes, which are more common in New Zealand. An indigenous type of clam called *toheroa* was adopted by British settlers for a soup that most Anglos would recognize as a form of clam chowder.

Influences also traveled in the opposite direction: after the British began planting wheat on the islands, Māori invented a sourdough bread called *rewena*. **Even the "national fruit" of New Zealand, the kiwi (right), originally came from China.**

FROM CLOSED TO OPEN

For centuries, Japan's attitude toward the world was described as *sakoku*, or "closed country." Very few foreigners were allowed in, and only very rarely were Japanese people allowed to travel out. *Sakoku* ended in the mid-1860s, and soon after Emperor Meiji began actively encouraging Japanese engagement with the world. In that period, a new cuisine was born: *yōshoku*, or "Western food."

Hayashi raisu is an iconic yōshoku concoction: a beef stew with red wine, onions, and mushrooms—essentially, a Japanese version of beef stew. *Naporitan* is a vaguely spaghetti-like dish made with ketchup, while *kareishu* is curried rice. (If you're thinking, "Wait, curry isn't Western" . . . you make a good point! But curry was brought from India to Britain and then to Japan, so in the eyes of early *yōshoku* chefs, it was just as Western as ketchup.)

These days, *yōshoku* dishes have been around so long and have evolved so much that they are no longer considered foreign. They're just another style of Japanese food.

OH CANADA!

Former Canadian prime minster Joe Clark once noted that "Canada has a cuisine of cuisines. Not a stew pot but a smorgasbord." Nowhere is that truer than in Canada's biggest cities, and Vancouver (below), on the west coast, is no exception. The city has a lively mix of restaurants, many of which take advantage of the city's comparative closeness to Asia. In fact, **the world's first Chinese buffet restaurant was founded in Vancouver's Gastown neighborhood in 1870**. Today, the city is home to some very unique fusion restaurants. Some favorite blends include Korean/Mexican, Japanese/Mexican, Asian/British pub food, and even Japanese/Italian.

Are You Going to Eat That?

What vegetables are in season? What protein sources are readily available? These are key questions for all cooks. But sometimes the available ingredients are . . . unexpected!

IT'S NOT JUST GOOD, IT'S OFFAL

The internal organs of the animals we eat (such as cows, sheep, and pigs) are called "offal." **Different cultures have different ideas about what to do with what writer and chef Anthony Bourdain once called "the nasty bits."**

- **Kidneys** (above right) are a commonly eaten organ. The British eat steak and kidney pie, while the French have many preparations for what they call *rognons*; the Spanish likewise eat a lot of *riñones*. Pork and kidney stew is called *hökarpanna* in Sweden.

- **The lining of animals' stomachs is called tripe.** In Serbia they've been making a tripe stew called *skembici* for hundreds of years. The Mexican version of tripe stew is called *menudo*, while *shkembe* is a tripe soup found in all countries with Persian influences, such as Iran and Turkey. In Florence, Italy, people enjoy a tripe sandwich called *lampredotto*.

- Humans have been cooking and eating the **tongues** (below) of their fellow mammals for more than 2 million years. Back then, it was wildebeest—today, it's most often cow (below) or pig. Some Texas ranchers encourage the eating of buffalo tongue, while specialty restaurants in Japan defy an international whaling ban to sell stewed whale tongue.

"NOPE" TIMES EIGHT

What are both some of the most-feared creatures and, apparently, also some of the most delectable? Spiders.

The Piaroa tribe in Venezuela roasts their tarantulas over an open fire, while Cambodians prefer their tarantulas fried. Street vendors in China sell roasted spiders on skewers, while in Thailand an adult-beverage manufacturer sells spider-infused vodka.

Scorpions are even more common than spiders in specialty alcohol, and they're also made into novelty candies. Chefs in Asian countries boil, grill, or fry their scorpions, which are very high in protein. Typically, the stinger and venom sac are removed before cooking, but that's not always true. In any case, heat usually renders the venom inactive, and it probably won't cause a fatal allergic reaction in humans (although that has happened).

JUST LIKE CHICKEN?

Lizards are a staple food in some indigenous cultures and are eaten as an exotic "treat" in others. For example, on the island of Luzon in the Philippines, two tribes—the Ilongot and the Aeta—both eat forest monitor lizards, which live in the trees and grow to as long as 6 ft (1.8 m). People in Honduras turn a particular species of iguana (below) into a soup, *consome de garrobo*; some Hondurans claim the soup can cure cancer and even wake the dead (*levantamuertos*). Meanwhile, **iguanas are so popular in Belize that they are known as "bamboo chicken."**

MONKEYING AROUND

People in Lesotho flavor their steaks with "monkey gland" sauce, while Danish children love a pasta dish called *abehjerne* (monkey brains). But there is no monkey in either of those dishes.

On the other hand, if you're offered "bushmeat stew" in Chad or Benin, there's likely some monkey in there. Of course, "bushmeat" is a generic term for any kind of wild animal hunted for food. Hunting these local animals has always been and continues to be an important aspect of life in rural Africa.

How Would You Like That Cooked?

From an open flame to a microwave, from a wok to a pressure cooker, there are tons of different ways to turn raw ingredients into a tasty dinner.

BAMBOO COOKING

Common throughout Asia and Pacific Rim countries, bamboo is technically a grass, but it's so much more than that. Not only is bamboo an excellent building material, it can also be made into furniture and clothing—and it can replace pots and pans! In Vietnam, Thailand, and other Southeast Asian countries, **food is packed into the hollow centers of bamboo and then grilled (above right)**. When cooked through, the bamboo can even be cut open and used as a serving dish. Bamboo shoots can themselves be eaten—they're frequently used in stir-fries and soups.

DOWN IN THE PIT

One of the oldest cooking techniques uses fire as the heat and the ground as the oven, and some cultures continue that tradition today. Native Hawaiians call this technique *kālua* (below). For a big celebration, or *lū'au*, hosts might prepare *kālua* pig or *kālua* turkey—either way, the meat is slow-cooked in a pit oven called an *imu*. The Maori of New Zealand have a similar tradition, which they call "putting down a *hāngi*." A *hāngi* involves heating rocks and burying them in a pit oven with meats and vegetables. Like a *lū'au*, a *hāngi* is reserved for special occasions.

THE CUTEST APPLIANCE

In 16th-century England, meat was cooked over a flame on a device called a turnspit. Some unlucky servant (usually the youngest male) had to stand by the roaring hot fire for hours, burning his hands on the iron handle and making that spit turn. Then in the late 1500s, things changed—turnspit dogs became the must-have kitchen appliance.

Turnspit dogs were small, short-legged canines that ran endlessly inside what was essentially a large hamster wheel, which was hung on the wall and connected to the spit. *Canis vertigus* **(dizzy dogs) were bred especially**

for the job and sold to kitchens all over the United Kingdom and, eventually, America. These downtrodden dogs looked a little bit like corgis (below)—ironic, given that today, corgis are the favorite dogs of the Queen of England.

By the late 1800s, turnspit dogs were replaced by machines. Which was a good thing—running on a wheel six days a week (Sundays off) couldn't have been a very enjoyable life. In fact, saving turnspit dogs from mistreatment was an early cause of the American Society for the Prevention of Cruelty to Animals (ASPCA).

Drink Up!

Humans can survive without food for three or four weeks, but without liquids we'll only last three or four days.

COFFEE AND TEA FOR YOU AND ME

According to the International Coffee Association, the United States is by far the most coffee-addicted nation in the world. In fact, the next in line doesn't even come close— **each year, Americans consume over 23,000 bags of coffee beans** (132 lbs or 60 kg each). That's more than twice the amount of the next-thirstiest country, Germany. Japan, France, and Italy round out the top five.

When it comes to tea, Turkey is by far the biggest consumer. The Food and Agriculture Organization reports that the average Turk consumes more than 26 pounds (over 12 kg) of tea per year. As with coffee, that's way beyond the next country, Russia (well over 8 lb or 4 kg per person).

THIS STINK'S FOR YOU

When you've reached an acceptable age for adult beverages, there are lots of options. Rather than reaching for a beer, how about some *kumis*, a **fermented horse milk** that's popular in Kyrgyzstan? It's called *airag* in Mongolia. Still not interested?

Or perhaps some Chinese snake wine is in order. **Snake wine** is made by putting a snake into a bottle of alcohol; the alcohol detoxifies the venom while, some believe, leaving the venom's medicinal properties behind. Vietnam also has snake wine, while in Japan there's a similar beverage—*habushu*, or snake sake. The same general concept underlies **scorpion tequila**, from Mexico.

If you're really adventurous, how about some **Inuit seagull wine**? Seagull wine is not made like snake wine or scorpion tequila, where an animal is placed into a bottle of preexisting alcohol. No, no. Seagull wine is made by taking a dead seagull, putting it in a bottle of water, and setting it in the sun to ferment. Care for some liquified, rotten seagull? Cheers!

I'D LIKE TO BUY THE WORLD A BIRD'S NEST

The invention of soda (or "pop," depending on where you're from) dates back to 1767, when Joseph Priestley figured out how to put carbon dioxide bubbles into water. These days, sodas are popular all over the world, but there are a lot of regional variations. Here are just a few:

- In the Bahamas, Goombay Punch is a popular soda that tastes like pineapple and lime.
- Thums Up is essentially the Coca-Cola of India.
- The Japanese soft-drink company Ramune has made some inroads in Western grocery stores (they're the ones with glass marbles in the bottles). But you have to go all the way to Japan to find Ramune's line of savory sodas, with flavors like chili oil, curry, and wasabi.
- Pakola is Pakistan's soda brand of choice—it comes in lychee and raspberry flavors.
- Tunisia's most popular soda is called Boga, and it comes in cider, lemon-lime, and mint flavors.
- **Vietnam's Bird Nest soda contains a fungus that literally comes from bird nests.** Supposedly it's a health drink, but in order to receive the benefits, you have to get past its chunky texture.

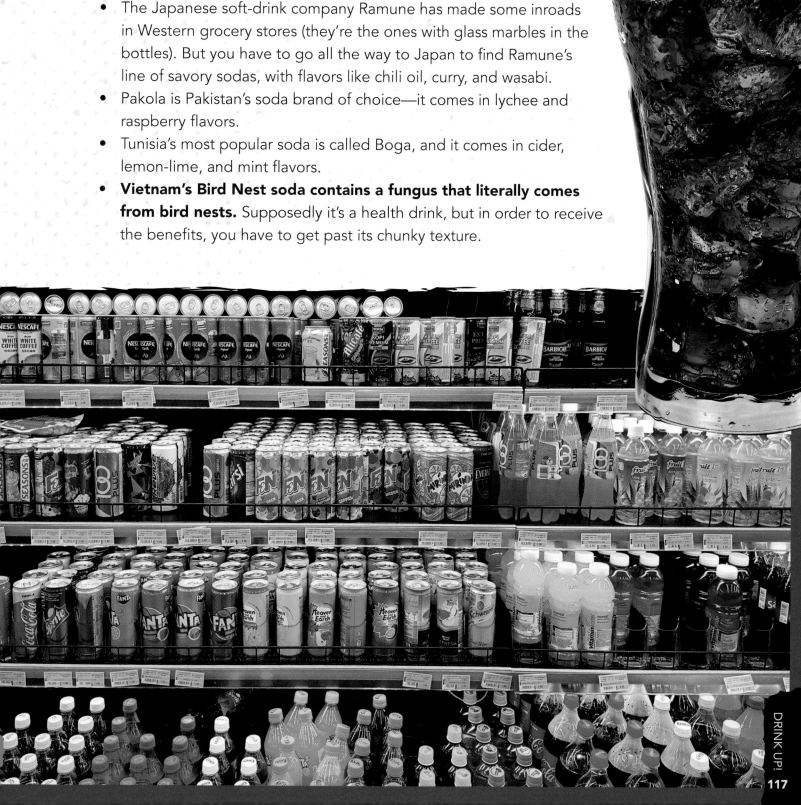

Mind Your Manners

We know, we know . . . *dining etiquette* sounds like a topic for a grouchy aunt. But there's a thin line between what's okay and what's *not-at-all* okay, and it can tell you a lot about a culture.

TAKE A SEAT

Pulling up a chair to your kitchen table may seem like a completely obvious way to begin a meal, but throughout much of the world, that's not how it's done. Across Asia and the Middle East, **meals are traditionally eaten while sitting on cushions on the floor.** For instance, in Afghanistan, people gather around the *dastarkhan*. The literal translation of *dastarkhan* is "tablecloth," but the word really refers to the entire practice

of having a communal meal around an array of dishes. It's important to sit correctly—exposing the bottom of your feet is considered extremely rude.

In Japan, it's traditional to kneel at the table, in a position called *seiza*. In informal situations, it's okay for men to sit cross-legged (*agura*) or for women to sit with their legs folded to one side (*yokozuwari*).

HOST FAIL?

In Western countries, the best dinner guests are the ones who "clean their plate." An empty plate shows that you enjoyed the meal, while leaving food behind suggests that you didn't like what you were given. But in other parts of the world, including both **Asian and South American countries, politeness requires you to leave a bit of food uneaten. A small amount of extra food on your plate is a signal that your host has provided everything you needed and slightly more.** An empty plate, on the other hand, suggests that your host failed and didn't give you enough to eat.

KEEP YOUR HANDS TO YOURSELF

In some parts of the world, it's natural to eat with your hands. Be careful which hand you use, though! From Fiji to Afghanistan and Sri Lanka to many countries in Africa, **the left hand is associated with . . . let's say . . . things you take care of in the bathroom**. Consequently, you never eat with that hand, regardless of how well you washed it.

PLATE PURITY

When serving food in Nepal, it's important that the serving utensils not touch any individual plates. This custom comes from concerns about purity and is common in many Hindu countries. A related rule is that once one person has started eating off a plate, no one else can eat off that plate. But that doesn't mean you can't share! In India, for example, sharing food is strongly encouraged— you just need to share from the serving dishes. **You don't share directly from your plate to the other person's**, and you would never reach across the table to sneak a bite of someone else's food.

SHHH!

Dining is an important social activity in most of the world's cultures—an opportunity not only to eat food but to connect with family and friends. That's not true in North Korea (right), however, where meals are fairly quiet affairs. People there believe the focus should be more on the food, less on distracting chit-chat.

Actually, there is a rather important exception to this rule. Before the meal can begin, everyone is expected to acknowledge the country's leaders, the Kim family. **Diners must express their thanks to the Kim portraits that are displayed in every North Korean home.**

Celebrating with Food

No matter where you go, it's just not a party without food, and sometimes the party *is* the food.

MONKEY SEE, MONKEY EAT

Lopburi City, Thailand (below), is known as "the city of monkeys," due to the large number of long-tailed macaques that live in the jungles nearby. Every year, the city celebrates an annual Monkey Buffet. Don't worry, though: **this is a buffet *for* monkeys, not *of* monkeys.**

On the last Sunday in November, the streets of Lopburi are lined with tables, which are laid out with more than 8,000 pounds (4,000 kg) of fruit, sticky rice, desserts, and flowers. The macaques are not afraid of humans and are happy to take a trip into town to enjoy the food—just be on your guard because hungry macaques will snatch anything that might be food, even if it's just your phone or your house keys.

CELEBRATION OF YAMS

Yams (left) are a vital ingredient in the cuisine of Nigeria and Ghana, and as a result, **yam season is cause for celebration**. Yams ripen in late summer, and the Igbo people celebrate the event with a festival called Iri-Ji (first-yam eating). There are parties, parades, and dances to honor the yam. By tradition, the oldest man in any given village eats the first yam of the season. It must be consumed during the festival, however— eating yams before the Iri-Ji celebration will bring bad luck.

SPECIAL RECIPE

In countries where Christianity is the majority religion, Christmas is arguably the most important holiday of the calendar. But in the rest of the world, December 25 is just another day. *Unless* you're in Japan, where **12/25 is marked with a dinner of Colonel Sanders's special KFC, or Kentucky Fried Chicken.** The tradition of dining on KFC for Christmas started in the early 1970s when American visitors went looking for a meal that at least vaguely resembled the turkey dinners they were missing back home. These days, Japanese people are so enthusiastic about KFC that they place their orders many days in advance, just to be sure that the extra-crispy isn't sold out when the moment arrives.

FOOD FIGHT

One of Spain's stranger festivals is La Tomatina (right), which takes place every year in the small town of Buñol. Normally home to fewer than 10,000 residents, every August the region swells with tourists, who've all traveled to Buñol in order to take place in a **massive outdoor tomato fight**. La Tomatina has been held every year since 1945 when an unrelated parade broke down into a frenzy of vegetable throwing. Since then, the food fight has focused exclusively on tomatoes, which need to be squashed by hand first, so that no one gets hurt. There are now similar tomato-throwing festivals in towns in China, Colombia, Costa Rica, India, and the United States.

Other countries have food-fight festivals that don't involve tomatoes, such as Ivrea, Italy's **"Battle of the Oranges,"** where residents reenact a rebellion that took place in 1194.

HOLIDAYS AND CELEBRATIONS

In Tokyo, Japan, the annual **CRYING SUMO FESTIVAL** centers on a competition involving two sumo wrestlers, each holding a baby. They carry the little ones into the ring, where each sumo tries to make the other sumo's baby cry—the loudest crier wins.

For as long as there have been communities, there have been celebrations of one kind or another. Whether you are celebrating a birthday, **INDEPENDENCE DAY**, or that special time of year when **JAPANESE PEOPLE THROW SOYBEANS AT EACH OTHER**, please enjoy these facts about **partying down**.

The largest single fireworks shell weighed 2,397 lbs (1,087 kg) and was fired by the United Arab Emirates as the climax of their 2018 New Year's celebrations.

One of the oldest holidays still observed is the Jewish festival of Passover (or Pesach, in Hebrew). **Passover celebrates the liberation of the Israelites from slavery in Egypt,** and it has been around for close to 3,000 years.

Happy Birthday to You!

No matter where you go, it's just not a party without food, and sometimes the party *is* the food.

NINETY—FIVE MILLION BIRTHDAYS

Sometimes it's fun when someone you know shares your birthday, but what if your entire country did?

Vietnamese people don't celebrate—or even pay much attention to—the literal date of their birth. Instead, every Vietnamese person gets a year older on Tet, which is Vietnamese New Year. It's been said that **Tet wraps** **Christmas, New Year's, and birthdays into one giant celebration**. Tet lasts for three to five days, depending on the community. There are family reunions, dragon dances (above), fireworks, and elaborate banquets. Children are given money in lucky red envelopes, but how much they get depends on how well behaved they've been, so watch yourself.

NO COW FOR YOU

In Benin (below), some birthdays are more important than others. A person's first, fifth, tenth, and fifteenth birthdays are celebrated to the hilt with parties that last all day and all night. There is a feast—often with an entire cow or goat as the main course—and gifts of flowers or money. Other birth years are also celebrated in Benin, but on a much smaller scale. Don't expect anybody to slaughter a cow for you when you turn twelve, okay?

С ДНЁМ РОЖДЕНИЯ!
(HAPPY BIRTHDAY!)

Russians have some very specific ideas about birthdays. In school when it's your birthday, you are expected to bring candy for everyone else in class. **Russians sometimes present the birthday celebrant with a personalized pie that has a message written on top.** But a more severe Russian tradition is that you must never celebrate your birthday *before* the actual date. If you do, you're basically tempting fate to kill you before you reach the birthday you celebrated too soon.

It used to be traditional for Russians to ignore their 40th birthday. The number 40 is associated with death, so it was considered a bad idea to make a big deal of being 40 years old. That tradition is rarely followed these days, however.

OTO THIS WORLD

A traditional birthday breakfast in Ghana is a dish called *oto*, which is a **Ghanaian yam (a variety of sweet potato) mashed and then fried in palm oil with hard-boiled egg on top**. A Ghanaian yam is very different from the type you might know. These yams are about as long as your arm and are covered in a thick, almost bark-like skin. *Oto* is also served to brides on their wedding day and to mothers of new babies. It's also offered as comfort food to people mourning the loss of a family member.

CELEBRATING AGE

As with many cultures around the world, a Mongolian child's first birthday is cause for a big celebration. After that, Mongolians (right) do things a bit differently from most. In the West, birthdays are usually most significant for children, while adults may ignore them; in Mongolia, on the other hand, **the older you become, the more you are celebrated.**

In the old days, Mongolian kids' birthdays were lumped together and celebrated at the first day of the closest lunar month. In contemporary Mongolia, however, it's becoming more common to have a very small birthday party on the actual date. But it's not until you get older that celebrations get more elaborate. A Mongolian's 61st birthday is cause for a big celebration, as is the 73rd. And if you make it to 85, look out: **it's party time!**

Happy Birthday to Us!

Most countries celebrate some form of independence or founder's day. After all, it's the moment that a country became itself!

INDEPENDENCE NOW, LIBERATION LATER

On March 1, South Korea celebrates Samil-jeol (above), which has a somewhat similar backstory to American Independence Day. On that day in 1919, Korean independence leaders gathered in a restaurant to read their Declaration of Independence from Japan, which ruled them at the time. They presented their signed document to the Japanese leaders, who promptly arrested them all. This sparked protests that resulted in the deaths of thousands of Koreans. **Their sacrifice is honored every year with bullfights (no actual bulls, though, just people dressed as bulls!)** and a public reading of the declaration.

FLY HIGH

India celebrates its independence from the British Empire every August 15. That's the day in 1947 when the first prime minister, Jawaharlal Nehru, unfurled the Indian flag for the first time. To mark that occasion, **kites in the colors of the flag (orange, white, and green) are flown all over the country.** The practice of kite flying (right) is very popular in India, where it's strongly associated with the spirit of independence.

WHEN DRACULA BECAME ROMANIAN

For a long time, Romania's major national holiday was May 1, marking the day Romania (below) declared independence from the Ottoman Empire in 1877. But when the country was reborn as the Socialist Republic of Romania in 1947, the national day was switched to August 23, celebrating the overthrow of the previous government. When the Socialist Republic was itself overthrown in 1989, the holiday was moved once again. These days, Romania's national holiday is Ziua Nationala (National Day), and it's held every December 1. It **marks the date that the previously independent state of Transylvania (the home of Dracula)** joined the states of Moldovia and Wallachia to form a united Romania.

BIRTH PAINS

The world's youngest country, South Sudan, voted to become independent from Sudan in January 2011. **Their official Independence Day, July 9, is celebrated with parades and festivals.**

The young country has been torn apart, riven by a civil war that started in 2013, causing the deaths of thousands and forcing millions of people to flee the country (mainly to nearby Uganda). What's more, the conflict has destroyed crops and brought oil production—South Sudan's only real export—to a virtual standstill, causing huge financial problems. In the face of all this turmoil, South Sudan's president was forced to cancel Independence Day celebrations in 2018.

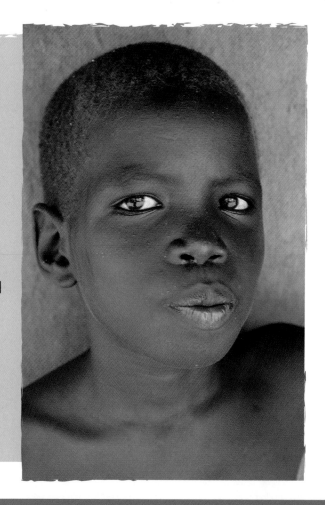

Ring in the New

Wherever, whenever, and however you celebrate, the beginning of the New Year is a fresh start for us all!

NEW YEAR, NEW JOY

In China, the *real* new year isn't on January 1. **Chinese New Year takes place sometime in late January or early February, depending on the lunar calendar.** It's marked by family gatherings, banquets, parades with dragon dances (right), and firework displays.

There are lots of legends surrounding the history of the holiday—one is that long ago, a monster named Nian (meaning "year") terrorized villages, destroying their crops and eating the livestock. But Nian was scared away by loud noises, bright lights, and, for some reason, the color red.

Homes are thoroughly cleaned (to wipe away the previous year) and then decorated with lots of red. Many people hang *chūn lián*, which are red banners printed with sayings like **"New year, new joy, and new century."** Wearing red clothing is also important, and children are given red envelopes containing money.

STOP EVERYTHING

Every year, the people of Bali mark their New Year (which falls in March, due to their calendar) with an extraordinary holiday called Nyepi Day, when the entire country stops everything it's doing and focuses solely on fasting and meditation (below). **On Nyepi Day, the rules are "no fire," "no travel," "no activity," and "no entertainment."** Total silence is observed. The Ngurah Rai International Airport shuts down, no one drives or goes to work, and when darkness falls, no one turns on any lights or makes fires. Even ATMs don't work—but of course, no one needs money because there's nothing to buy. As a cafe owner described it to a reporter, Nyepi is "the day for contemplation, to meditate, to fast, to go inside yourself and reflect on the past year. People stay quietly with their families, it's a very special day."

SMASH IT UP

In Denmark, it's traditional to go out on New Year's Eve and **smash old plates against the front doors of your friends** and loved ones. When you wake up on New Year's Day, finding a lot of broken plates is a sign that you have tons of friends.

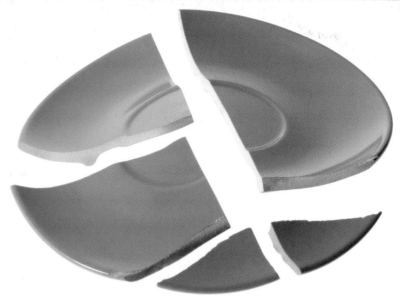

SHAKING THE HOUSE

The Persian New Year is called Nowruz (New Day), and it's celebrated on the first day of spring, which falls on or near March 21. Nowruz is principally celebrated in Iran but also all over Central Asia and in parts of the Middle East. Spring cleaning is a big part of the Nowruz tradition—it's called *khooneh tanooki* (shaking the house). **There's even a Santa Claus–like character called Amoo, who wears red and brings presents to kids.**

HOT NEW YEAR'S PARTIES

In New Zealand (and the rest of the Southern Hemisphere), the New Year comes at the height of summer, not winter. To enjoy the weather, there are lots of festivals all over the country, such as the Aum New Year Festival outside Auckland, the free concert at the Whairepo Lagoon in Wellington, or the Highlife New Year's Eve event on Waiheke Island. But **New Zealanders who prefer to keep it simple just go outside and bang pots and pans to make as much racket as possible.**

Unique Celebrations

Some cultures have their own unique holidays that you'll find nowhere else.

LANDLOCKED ARMADA

Holidays usually celebrate some sort of victory or happy occasion. But every **March 23 Bolivia observes the national holiday Dia del Mar (Day of the Sea), which mourns the now-landlocked country's loss of its coast.**

The War of the Pacific (1879–1883) pitted Bolivia and Peru against Chile for control of the Atacama Desert—the only spot where Bolivia had access to the sea. In the end, Bolivia lost the territory, but they gained a national hero in Eduardo Abaroa. When Chilean forces told him to surrender, Abaroa famously replied, **"Surrender, me?! Tell your grandmother to surrender!"**

Bolivians have not surrendered the idea that they'll get that coastline back one day. They've even kept a star on their coat of arms that signifies "El Litoral" (The Shore), which they feel still belongs to them. On El Dia del Mar, the anniversary of Abaroa's death, there are parades where bands play songs about the Pacific Ocean and the Bolivian Armada (which, yes, is a real thing).

SOMEBODY SAVE QU YUAN

China's major summer holiday is called Duanwu, but it's better known around the world as the Dragon Boat Festival (left).

Originally, the holiday honored the legendary poet and politician Qu Yuan, who lived around 300 BCE. He was exiled for political reasons and attempted to kill himself by jumping in a river. Friends and political allies leapt into boats, hoping to save him—which is why he is honored today by dragon-boat races—but they couldn't. Instead, they dropped bits of rice into the river, hoping the fish would eat the rice rather than their friend's body. This is said to be the real inspiration for *zongzi* (sticky rice wrapped in bamboo), which is the traditional meal during Duanwu. **Today, the Dragon Boat Festival is a major sporting event in China with racers from many countries traveling to compete.**

HAPPY CARPET DAY!

Say what you will about Turkmenistan's autocrats, but they do love their made-up holidays.

Turkmenistan observes about two dozen different public holidays, many of which were invented out of thin air by the country's first president (read: dictator) Saparmurat Niyazov.

For example, **the first Sunday in April is Grain of Gold, Drop of Water Day**. The holiday, such as it is, centers on a speech by the country's leader on the always-festive subject of water-resource management. The country also marks its agricultural and industrial exports with their own holidays, such as Carpet Day (above), Melon Day, and every child's favorite, Day of the Employees of the Oil and Gas, Energy, and Geological Industries.

HERITAGE AND RECONCILIATION

Countries use national holidays to honor their history, and sometimes to recover from it. South Africa observes numerous national holidays relating to their uniquely painful history of apartheid, a policy of racial segregation that exploited people of color and denied them basic human rights.

March 21 used to be called Sharpeville Day, in honor of the 69 people who were killed by police during a protest; these days the national holiday is called Human Rights Day instead. **April 27 is Freedom Day, marking the anniversary of the country's first free elections in 1994.** September 24 is Heritage Day, which is meant to celebrate the diversity of all the different ethnic groups that make up the country. And December 16 is Reconciliation Day, which aspires to celebrate the coming together of all South Africans as one nation.

Fabulous Festivals

Around the world, people gather to enjoy cultural festivities—some amazing, and some amazingly weird.

I'LL GIVE YOU SOMETHING TO CRY ABOUT

Parents usually spend their time trying to keep their children from crying, but not at the Crying Sumo Festival (left). A contest held every April at multiple shrines in Tokyo, Japan, the competition involves two sumo wrestlers, each holding a baby. They carry the little ones into the ring, where **each sumo tries to make the other sumo's baby cry—the loudest crier wins**. While this may seem cruel, the tradition intends to scare away demons and give the babies good luck in life. According to an old Japanese saying, "Naku ko wa sodatsu," which means, "The crying child grows fast."

OOMPAH AFRICA

Beer and bratwurst aren't things you'd normally associate with southern Africa. But when German settlers went to Namibia in the 1840s, they brought the Oktoberfest beer festival tradition with them. **Every year the city of Winhoek (right), the nation's capital, is decorated to look like a Bavarian town**, and residents enjoy not only beer and sausages but lots of traditional music, which Namibians know as "oompah."

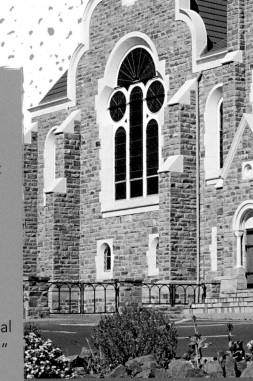

CHAM DANCES

Buddhist festivals in the kingdom of Bhutan are called *tshechus*, and they date back to the 1600s when Bhutan was united as a country. They're held at monasteries all over the country at various times of year. *Tshechus* honor Padmasambhava, a founder of Tibetan Buddhism, who is also called Guru Rimpoche or "the second Buddha."

The central event of *tshechus* are masked dances called *cham* dances (left). Depending on the particular festival, **cham dances can be performed by monks and nuns**, lay people, or in some instances even soldiers. *Cham* dances teach about Buddhism and also constitute a form of blessing for the audience. *Cham* dances are also performed in Tibet and India.

FLY AWAY HOME

Many countries have holidays to honor the dead—think Día de los Muertos (Day of the Dead) in Mexico, which celebrates the annual return of departed souls to visit their living relatives. But Guatemalans have a unique way of connecting with their ancestors. In parts of Guatemala, **people dress in traditional Mayan costumes and go to their local graveyards with kites for Barriletes Gigantes (Giant** Kite) festivals (below). Kite makers, called *barrileteros*, build amazing constructions from cloth, paper, and bamboo. **Some are as big as 65 feet (20 m) across.** The kites are flown as a way of connecting the next world to our own. Some of the kites carry messages that people hope to pass on to their relatives in the afterlife, while others are woven with political mottos to share with the living, like "Respect all life."

Taking It to the Streets

Call it what you want—a march, a procession, a second line. Everybody loves a parade!

YOU'D BETTER SALUTE!

A military presence at parades is common all over the world. **But true "military parades," specifically to show off armies and weaponry, are rare among Western democracies.** Not so in authoritarian countries, which have them fairly regularly. Russia held its largest-ever military parade in 2015, with about 16,000 soldiers, hundreds of armored vehicles, helicopters, and other hardware. The same year, China held a military parade with around 12,000 soldiers. On the opposite end of the spectrum, the tiny African country of Djibouti, hosts a military parade every year, even though their entire military is only 16,000 troops total. And of course, North Korea has military parades regularly—for national holidays, political birthdays, or just to show off a shiny new intercontinental ballistic missile.

EVERYBODY SECOND LINE

Folks in New Orleans, Louisiana (NOLA), don't wait for some special occasion to have a parade. **At any given moment, you can easily stumble into a parade called a "second line."** The name comes from the people who dance behind a brass band—the band is the "main line," and the dancers are the "second line." Anybody can throw a parade in NOLA, for literally any reason.

MILES AND MILES OF MARKSMEN

The prize for longest parade is claimed by Hanover, Germany, which hosts an annual Schützenfest (Marksmen's Fair) in early July (left). **The Grand Parade of the Marksmen features more than 10,000 marchers and over 100 bands.** The parade is about 7.5 miles (12 km) long, snaking through central Hanover to the fairgrounds.

PRIDE (IN THE NAME OF LOVE)

Parades celebrating the LGBTQ community (right) date back to the **Christopher Street Liberation Parade,** held in New York City in 1970. It marked the one-year anniversary of the Stonewall Riots, the beginning of the modern gay-rights movement. Today, pride parades are a global phenomenon, from Serbia to Mauritius and from Greenland to Taiwan.

The world's largest pride parade is probably Brazil's Parada do Orgulho LGBT de São Paulo with over 5 million participants. The Tel Aviv Pride Parade is the largest in the Middle East with some 150,000 participants every year.

Pride parades aren't accepted everywhere. In 2015, a parade in Ankara, Turkey, was violently dispersed. Likewise, the LGBTQ community in Uganda is highly persecuted, and their many attempts at holding events have been crushed. But Russia really took the lead when it comes to anti-pride; in 2012, the government declared a *100-year ban* on pride parades.

THAT'S A LOT OF *FLORES*

Every August, flower farmers in the area surrounding Medellín, Colombia, get their own parade, called Desfile de Silleteros (Flower Parade) (right). **The order of the parade marchers is determined by a flower arranging competition**—makers of the winning *silletas* (flower arrangements) march first. Originally, the word *silletas* referred to the method of carrying the flowers, but the word now refers to the entire arrangement. When we say "arrangement," understand that *silletas* are no clump of roses. One category of *silletas* is called "monumental," and those displays can be 13 feet (4 m) high and weigh as much as 220 pounds (100 kg).

Rockets' Red Glare

Ever since the days of medieval China, it's not truly a party without some explosions of color.

SPARKLING CELEBRATIONS

From the very beginning fireworks have been used to **scare evil spirits and welcome good luck.** So it's natural that fireworks are central to New Year's Eve, when cultures all over the world celebrate the opportunity for a fresh start. As the clock strikes twelve, spectacular fireworks displays can be seen above cities all over the world, whether in Auckland or Berlin, Jakarta or Beirut, Reykjavik or Kuala Lumpur.

SPARKLING CELEBRATIONS

Ultimately fireworks are just a question of chemistry. **Different compounds are combined to produce different colors.** And although China gets the bulk of the credit for the invention of fireworks, it was actually Italians who figured out which chemicals would produce which colors.

Next time you see a fireworks show, here's a handy guide to the compounds combusting over your head.

- Blue: copper
- Yellow: sodium
- Red: strontium or lithium
- Green: chlorine plus barium
- Turquoise: chlorine plus copper
- Silver: titanium or magnesium
- Orange: calcium

HOW DID THEY DO THAT?

The most amazing aspect of fireworks is probably the shapes they make. How is it possible to fire a bunch of shells into the sky that will explode in exactly the right formation? It all has to do with how the little pellets inside the fireworks shells are packed together—**the pattern the pellets make when they are assembled will be reflected in the shape the firework makes when it goes off.**

FIREWORKS FACTS

THE FIRST FIREWORKS show in England was held in honor of the wedding of King Henry VII to Elizabeth of York in 1486, which also marked the end of the Wars of the Roses.

THE JAPANESE WORD FOR FIREWORKS IS *HANABI*. July and August are big months for what are called *hanabi taikai* (fireworks show). There are several hundred, at least one a day somewhere in the country.

THE RECORD FOR LARGEST FIREWORKS show is held by the Philippines where 810,904 separate fireworks were set off in 2016. Second place goes to Dubai whose 2014 New Year's show set off around 500,000 separate fireworks in six minutes flat, at a cost of $6 million.

SCHOOL AND WORK

The word "school" comes from an ancient Greek word that meant leisure. Wait, what?! It's true. **The Ancient Greeks were so excited about education** that their idea of a good time was listening to lectures at the local *skholē*.

The hardest-working country in the world, according to the Organisation for Economic Cooperation and Development is **Mexico**, whose **citizens work the largest number of hours every year**, followed by Costa Rica as a close second and South Korea third.

The **world's largest school** is the British-style City Montessori School in Lucknow, India, which has some **32,000 students!**

The hardest-working country in Europe is the one descended from the folks who thought *school* and *fun* were the same thing: **Greece**.

School Days

Kids all over the world have school in common, but that doesn't mean all schools are the same.

MAKING THE GRADE

How'd you do on yesterday's test? Did you get an A? A 7? Or only a *media media*? Here's a sampling of grading systems from around the world:

- Brazil uses a 1 to 10 scale: 10 is the best (*superior superior*), 5 is just getting by (*media media*), and 0 is trouble (*sin rendimiento*).
- Djibouti schools have a 20-point scale: above 14 is high honors, above 12 is honors, 10 is a passing grade, and below 10 is failing.
- German grades range from 1 to 6: 1 is the best (*sehr gut*), 4 is fine (*ausreichend*), and 6 is failing (*ungenügend*).
- Mali grades on a scale of 1 to 20: 8 is the minimum to pass, while 15 and above is considered excellent.
- Tajikistan has a descriptive grading system with no numbers. An *a'lo* means you are really killing it, while *kanoatkakhsh* means you're doing fine, and *kom'eb* indicates you are barely squeaking by.

HOMEWORK OR NO WORK?

Students in Finland regularly top all other Europeans when it comes to their test scores. Guess how many hours young Finns spend on homework.

Zero. Zero hours per week.

On average, Finnish students have no homework. They also have shorter school days, and kids in elementary school get to play longer at recess—75 minutes per day on average, as opposed to 27 minutes on average in the United States.

How do the Finns do it? It may have something to do with the large number of teachers (1 teacher for every 12 students).

WHAT'S FOR LUNCH?

In many countries, the midday meal is the most important one, and it's common for kids to have classes in the morning, go home to eat with their families, and then go back to school in the afternoon. But lots of other schools do provide lunches—sometimes because it's a boarding school, other times because students travel quite a distance every day to get there.

Here's a sampling of a few typical foods served to students around the world:

- **Democratic Republic of the Congo:** fufu (starchy paste made from yam and cassava roots, kind of like mashed potatoes), stewed greens, caterpillars
- **Finland:** pea soup, beets, carrots, pannakkau (sweet pancake) with berries
- **Japan:** udon (noodle) soup, chikuwa (fish sausage), rice, vegetables
- **South Korea:** fish soup, kimchi (spicy, fermented vegetables), fresh vegetables, tofu, rice
- **Spain:** shrimp, rice, peppers, gazpacho (cold tomato soup)
- **Ukraine:** borscht (beet soup), sausage, mashed potatoes, shredded cabbage

SCHOOL FACTS

MANY JAPANESE STUDENTS like "good-luck" bracelets, but they aren't allowed to wear more than one at one time— too much luck could be considered cheating.

IN DENMARK, kids celebrate their fourth birthday by attending preschool for the first time.

IN ICELAND, a common class is knitting.

CHINESE STUDENTS in many schools are allowed to take naps on their desks after lunch.

Unique Schools

Schools don't need to be big brick buildings. They can be outdoors or online, or they can even float.

FLOATING SCHOOLS

In Southeast Asia, the country of Bangladesh experiences regular flooding, and not only during its "rainy season" from June to September. One result of all the floods was a lot of missed school days. To address this, **Bangladesh has about 100 boat schools (right).** They pick up kids in the morning, dock for the school day, and then bring them back home—basically, the boat schools are both bus and school in the same place. They even have solar-powered Internet access on board.

QUEENSLAND, YOU'RE ON THE AIR

Australia is home to vast stretches of difficult terrain, and people sometimes live hundreds of miles away from the nearest school. As a result, Australia offers the **School of the Air**, an Internet-based home-schooling program. Kids can log in from wherever they are to see their lessons and then take quizzes online. There's also a toll-free number kids can call to speak with their teachers directly. Parents periodically hold gatherings for kids in the same region, so that they can meet each other. And every year there's a camp, where students of School of the Air spend a week meeting and studying together in person.

School of the Air sounds pretty high-tech now, but it hasn't always been that way. **When the program began in the 1950s, it was all done by means of radio broadcasts.**

SCHOOL ANYWHERE

India is home to a number of extraordinary schools. The world's largest school is there—the British-style City Montessori School in Lucknow has some 32,000 students!

On the other side of the spectrum, in 1985 the educator Inderjit Khurana began the first "train platform school" in hopes of offering some form of education to the many impoverished kids sent out to beg on train platforms in major cities. Today **Khurana's organization runs 12 train-platform schools** and several "schools on wheels" that circulate in impoverished neighborhoods. A similar effort from teacher Rajesh Kumar Sharma offers basic classes for poor kids under a busy underpass in New Delhi—there's a boys' class that lasts for two hours every morning, and a girls' class for two hours in the afternoon.

WITCHCRAFT AND WIZARDING SCHOOLS

In the Harry Potter universe, there are seven wizarding schools, including one in Brazil, Japan, Uganda, and other places. The real world doesn't offer quite as many options, but that doesn't mean there are no opportunities for the magically inclined.

The College of Wizardry in Leśna, Poland, is a live-action role-play school held in a Harry Potter-esque castle. In the United Kingdom, the **Bothwell School of Witchcraft offers the same kind of role-playing experience**. Both "schools" offer weekend-long opportunities for Muggles to play out their fantasies.

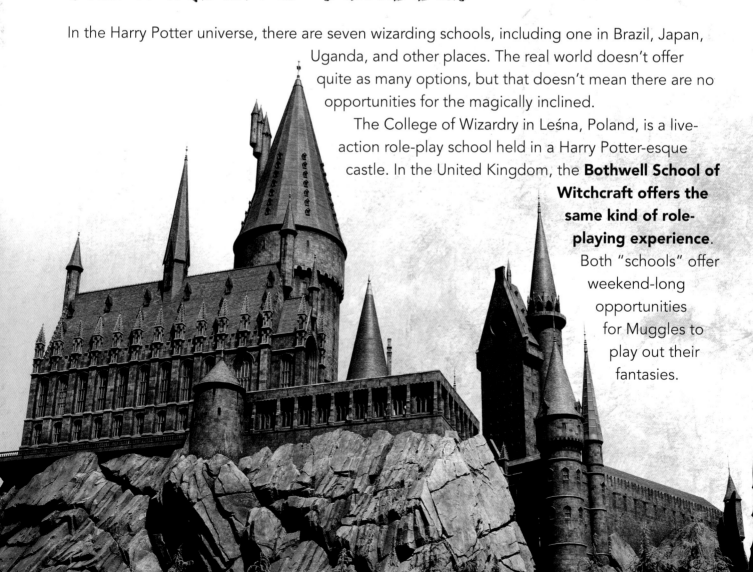

Hitting the Books

**Once you get to school, what do you study?
Turns out, a lot depends on where you are!**

TAKE ME TO YOUR LEADER

In North Korea (below) students must learn a foreign language, usually either **English or Chinese.** It's not clear who they'll be speaking with, since North Koreans are generally not allowed to travel, and tourism is tightly restricted. Still, language study is considered important because, as a repeated maxim goes, **"Foreign language is a weapon for life and struggle."**

FOLLOWING THE HERD

Mongolia requires kids go to school from ages 5 to 15, but about **30 percent of Mongolians are nomadic herders (right).** That makes it tricky for kids to stay in school all year. Kids of nomadic families sometimes have to go live with relatives so that they can continue their studies. Sometimes Mom stays in the *saum* (village) with the children while Dad travels with their animals. There's a lot of debate in Mongolia about whether nomadic kids should attend boarding school so that they don't miss out on their studies; some argue the separation from their families at a young age is a bad idea.

Whatever the challenges, education in Mongolia seems to work: **literacy rates are 98 percent for men and 98.9 for women.** When they begin 5th grade, Mongolian students begin studying either Russian or English or sometimes both.

GOING UP TO THE COUNTRY

For decades, schools in Havana, Cuba, had a unique educational program called Escuela al Campo (School in the Country). **For several months, groups of students from the city were sent out to boarding schools in agricultural areas.** Their days were split between tending crops in the morning and traditional classroom study in the afternoon. Fans of Escuela al Campo argued that the program taught practical skills while inspiring students to respect the dignity of manual labor.

Critics complained, however, that not only was student progress interrupted by the program, the kids were poorly treated, forced to work in fields without proper equipment or even shoes. In recent years, the Cuban government has been quietly dismantling the Escuela al Campo system.

THIS IS OUR COUNTRY

The Democratic Republic of the Congo (DRC) has a nationwide curriculum that all schools are expected to follow. Because the country was run by Belgium for a long time, both the subjects and the methods of teaching were heavily influenced by Belgian ideas about education. In recent years, the curriculum has been adjusted to better reflect what the people of the DRC think is important. That includes more religious topics; more emphasis on the arts, especially singing and music; and Congolese history. Students can also study African languages—**there are more than 200 languages spoken in the DRC**—but they still study French, as well.

See Me After Class

Countries around the world take many different approaches to extracurricular activities.

LE CLUB DE HOMEWORK

Most after-school clubs are designed to be fun, but . . . not all of them! For instance, most French schools offer **after-school homework clubs**, where kids can get help with their work before going home. These clubs, which are supposed to be managed by retired teachers or college students, are intended to solve the problem of parents not having time to help their children with their work.

That said, some members of the French government have suggested that **homework be banned completely**! Right now, that's just in the proposal stage. For the time being, homework club it is!

THE WAY OF BASEBALL

In the baseball-mad country of Japan, lots of kids spend their free time on the baseball diamond. But kids' baseball in Japan is quite different from what you might think. For one thing, **weekend practices can run as long as 8 to 10 hours at a stretch on both days!** Masumi Omae, who coaches one of the country's most successful little league teams, told a reporter that the word for this is *konjo*, which means tenacity. *Yakyudo*, or "the way of baseball," involves lots of discipline, repetition, and absolutely no egos or star players.

QUEEN OF KATWE

In Katwe, an extremely poor neighborhood in the Ugandan capital of Kampala, a man named Robert Katende started an amazing program as part of the Sports Outreach Institute. **He began teaching some of Uganda's poorest kids how to play chess**—a game so foreign to them that there's no word for it in their native language. It can't even be called an "after-school" club, because many kids who play chess there aren't able to afford school. And yet, one of Coach Robert's students, Phiona Mutesi, went on to represent Uganda in chess matches all over the world. She's even recognized as a Woman Candidate Master by the World Chess Federation. **Phiona's story was made into a fun movie called *The Queen of Katwe* in 2016**.

CRAM IT IN

In both Taiwan and mainland China (below), it's not unusual for students to spend their "free time" in *buxiban*. **Buxiban are tutorial centers—sometimes referred to as "cram schools"**—where students work on improving their skills in a wide variety of subjects, including math, science, and even art. The most popular *buxibans* are those that teach English. So after-school activities in China are basically just more school!

Nice Work, if You Can Get It

Let's check out the world's most unique jobs. . . .

CRYING ON CUE

If there were a prize for "country with weirdest jobs," Japan would win. Here's a sample of the unique ways people make a living in Japan.

- *Oshiya*, or pushers, are white-gloved men who **push people into Tokyo's overcrowded subway trains (right)**. They keep the crowds moving along and make sure everyone stands clear of the closing doors.
- If crowded trains stress you out, consider renting an *Ikemeso Danshi*, which means "handsome boy who weeps." He'll watch sad movies with you and wipe the tears from your cheeks.
- But if you're going to pay someone to cry with you, why not go all the way and **rent a boyfriend** (*Rentaru Kareshi*)? Agencies charge between $40 and $50 per hour.
- If your rental boyfriend offends someone, you can **hire a professional to apologize on your behalf**. Fees are determined by the apology format—emails are cheapest, in-person apologies are most expensive. One service offers "apology while crying," but they won't say how much *that* specialty costs.

NIGHT-NIGHT

When Hotel Finn in Helsinki, Finland, was due to reopen after a long period of renovations, the hotel owner knew he needed to do something special to publicize the event. He placed job advertisements looking for a **"professional sleeper"** to stay in the hotel for about a month and report about the comfort-level of each room, one at a time.

By the time you read this, the Helsinki job has been taken. But never fear: mattress companies and sleep labs all over the world also offer opportunities for professional sleepers. The Texas-based company MattressFIRM calls them **"snoozeterns."**

A MAN, A HORSE, SOME SHRIMP

In the western part of Belgium, on the North Sea, lies Oostduinkerke, where you'll find the world's only **horseback shrimpers (below)**. Following a tradition that dates back roughly 500 years, these Belgian fishermen ride their horses out into the water with nets attached to their saddles.

Unfortunately, there's reason for worry that the tradition may not last much longer. As the sea has warmed, the fishermen are catching far fewer shrimp and far more jellyfish, which can't be sold for food. Even so, many of the fishermen wouldn't have any other job. As Xavier Vanbillemont told a reporter, **"Ships can catch a lot more shrimps than me, but I prefer fishing with my horse, because he's my best friend."**

WEIRD JOB FACTS

MOST FORTUNE COOKIES come from one company, Wonton Food, which is the largest distributor of fortune cookies in the United States. And the fortunes were written by one man, Donald Lau, for about 30 years. He announced his retirement in 2017 due to a bad case of writer's block.

THE JOB OF "PROFESSIONAL PRINCESS" involves wearing costumes and entertaining kids on cruises and in amusement parks.

THE GIANT PANDA Breeding Research Center in Ya'an, China, hires "panda nannies" to hang out with the pandas and keep them occupied. A job opening in 2013 received about 100,000 applications.

Someone's Gotta Do It

Do you have what it takes to survive these dangerous jobs?

KEEPING YOUR HEAD

If you picture Thailand's Samphran Elephant Ground and Zoo, and you try to imagine who has the worst job, you might guess it's the guy who cleans up after all those elephants. That's not a bad guess, but the zoo does have worse jobs.

You see, Samphran doesn't only house elephants; it's also **home to about 10,000 crocodiles**. Twice a day there's a crocodile show at the zoo in which **stuntmen put their hands and, yes, even their heads in the crocs' mouths (above)**. Given that crocodiles have the strongest bite on Earth, all it would take is one annoyed saltwater crocodile to turn a "fun" show into a very, very bad day at the office.

A DEADLY TREK

When Westerners decide to scale the heights of Mount Everest (below), in the Himalayan mountains, they don't do it alone. In addition to a whole lot of cash—the license alone costs about $11,000 and that's before travel and equipment—they'll need to bring along a Sherpa.

Over the years, the word "sherpa" has become a regular noun, but actually **Sherpas are an ethnic group in Nepal and parts of India and China**. The name derives from their language and means "eastern people"—not, as you might assume, "somebody who carries your stuff."

On Everest, injury and death arrive in many forms, including but not limited to **falls**, **avalanches**, and **hypothermia**. Of all the deaths that have been recorded on Himalaya climbs, about one-third have been Sherpas. In a single 2014 avalanche, 14 Sherpas were killed.

DANGEROUSLY TIDY

On the surface, Rwanda's capital city, Kigali (below), is sparkling. Unlike many cities, the streets are clean and free of litter. Kigali has garbage containers at regular intervals and flowers planted along roads. But according to some reports, there is an ugly underside to that attractive exterior.

A small army of women work long hours, six days a week, cleaning the streets with nothing but straw brooms. They don't have reflective clothing, not even when sweeping highways where cars zoom by at top speed—sometimes missing the women by mere inches. For this most dangerous of jobs, the women streetsweepers are reported to earn about $70 per month.

IN RUSSIA, SMOKE JUMPS ON YOU

Firefighting is well known to be among the world's most dangerous jobs. And the most dangerous firefighting job has got to be smokejumping, which involves **parachuting directly into the middle of forest fires**. Smokejumping was invented by Russians in the 1930s, and to this day the country still employs the most smokejumpers in the world.

Russian smokejumpers do this dangerous job in the most dangerous ways possible—with old equipment, minimal safety regulations, and no seatbelts whatsoever. "We face danger three times," one smokejumper told a National Geographic reporter, "one when we fly on plane; two when we jump; three when we go to fire."

ARTS AND ENTERTAINMENT

The arts are how we express who we are. Whatever your favorite art form might be, there are probably people in other countries, thousands of miles away, who **love IT JUST AS YOU DO.**

In Saudi Arabia, all forms of **Pokémon** are banned for religious reasons.

Considered the national dance of Brazil, Capoeira (left) is a blend of dancing, martial arts, and acrobatics that formed among African slaves, mainly from what's now Angola. Capoeira might have developed because the slaves hid their fighting skills by disguising the moves as dance.

India's movie industry, known as Bollywood, releases more than 1,600 films per year—that's nearly four times as many as Hollywood.

Music

Whether they listen around a campfire or through an online streaming service, music is a fundamental part of people's lives all over the world.

TWO IN ONE

How many different notes can you sing at the same time? Just one? You must not be a throat-singer. **Throat-singing is an ancient technique** that uses special breathing, along with exact movements of the tongue and larynx, to create multiple notes at the same time. Throat-singers can essentially harmonize with themselves. The best-known throat singers are in Tuva (above), which is a part of Russia near Mongolia. The Xhosa people of South Africa and the Inuit of northern Canada also have long throat-singing traditions.

MUSIC TO FLOAT BY

Typical mariachi bands (below) have violins, brass instruments such as trumpets, and a pair of guitars, one with five strings and one with six. **Their costumes are called *traje de charros*, and the look is inspired by cowboys in the Mexican state of Jalisco**.

   The best place in the world to see and hear mariachis is probably the canals of Xochimilco, a neighborhood in Mexico City. Boats called *trajinera* travel up and down the canals, some carrying full mariachi bands that serenade tourists as they float along.

ANYTHING YOU CAN DO, I CAN DO WEIRDER

Demons playing heavy metal . . . a giant hamster wheel . . . a rapping turkey puppet. It can only be the Eurovision Song Contest (below).

One of the biggest—and some would say silliest—events in global pop music is the annual Eurovision Song Contest. The first contest was held in 1956, and only 10 European countries competed. The contest has gotten bigger and splashier ever since, with additional countries competing each year—a record 43 countries entered in 2018.

Eurovision is known for its **over-the-top performances**: the demons (below) were Finland's entry in 2006, the hamster wheel was courtesy of Ukraine in 2014, and the rapping turkey was the brainchild of Ireland's 2008 team. Ireland has scored top prize a remarkable seven times, but the year of the hip-hop turkey was not one of them.

MUSIC FACTS

BRASS BANDS are popular in India, and there's at least one non-Indian song that every brass band knows: "Tequila."

THE DIDGERIDOO (below) is an ancient instrument of the indigenous people of Australia. There are cave paintings showing didgeridoos that are about **1,500 years old**.

FÊTE DE LA MUSIQUE or Music Day is celebrated every June 21. The tradition began in Paris but is now **celebrated in more than 100 countries**. Free concerts are held, and people are encouraged to go outside and play or listen to music.

Dance

Since the first belly dance some 6,000 years ago, dances have come in two basic flavors. One is theatrical ("you sit over there and watch me dance") and the other is social ("we'll all dance together"). Within those categories, there are an infinite variety of ways and reasons to get up and dance.

EVERYBODY JUMP!

In parts of Kenya and Tanzania, young Maasai warriors go through a four-day ritual called *eunoto* (right), in which they graduate from junior status to senior warriors, who are able to marry. **A central part of eunoto ceremonies is a dance called *adumu***, which means "jump." Participants stand in a circle and sing while the young men take turns jumping in the circle—the key is to keep the body completely straight and jump as high as possible without letting your heels touch the ground. These days, *adumu* is also performed informally, mostly for tourists.

FREE MEN KICKING

The Cossacks are an ethnic group in parts of what are now Russia, Poland, and Ukraine. Their community dates back to the 15th century when people fled oppression under the serf system (a type of forced labor from the Middle Ages). Appropriately, the word *cossack* means "free man." The Cossacks became known as expert horsemen and fierce warriors-for-hire.

   Cossacks are also dancing machines. Their style features energetic squat-kicks, performed while spinning in circles (right). It also features tumbling and acrobatics, sometimes while holding swords. The Cossack style also influenced other regional dances. The Russian *kazachok* has a similar squat-kick step, while the dance of Georgian shepherds, *khanjluri*, features spinning on your knees while throwing daggers.

CHOOSE LIFE, CHOOSE CAPOEIRA

Ringing the city of Rio de Janeiro, Brazil, are overcrowded, crime-ridden neighborhoods called favelas. For kids who grow up there, it can be very hard to break the cycle of violence all around them. Some **groups, such as Awaken Capoeira, offer dance workshops in the favelas to instill cultural pride**.

Capoeira (right) is a blend of dancing, martial arts, and acrobatics that developed among African slaves, mainly from what's now Angola. The high-energy dance/fight style is now practiced all over the world and considered to be the national dance of Brazil. Groups like Awaken Capoeira hope to show favela youth that there's more to life than the gangs that rule their neighborhoods.

TINIKLING

In the Philippines, tinikling dancers (right) do fancy footwork in between two bamboo poles held lengthwise along the ground. Dancers are imitating a bird called the tikling, which has a particularly graceful manner of avoiding the traps set for it by farmers. Tinikling is **the national dance of the Philippines**. In addition to being performed in traditional contexts, these days it's also taught in exercise classes, the way aerobic dance is in the West.

"HEYYYY, MACA— WAIT, WHAT?!"

Wherever you roam across this beautiful blue marble, if you attend a wedding, bar mitzvah, or any party with group dancing, you can't avoid the Macarena (left). The gesture-based dance is performed to an infernally catchy song by Spanish lounge-singing duo Los del Rio. Originally released in 1992, **the song and accompanying goofball dance became a worldwide craze** in the mid-1990s. The Macarena is so simple that anyone can do it, and everyone probably has. What most people don't realize is that the song—which, keep in mind, is a staple of wedding receptions—celebrates a young woman who repeatedly cheats on her boyfriend while he's serving in the military.

Um . . . congratulations to the happy couple?

Movies

Who invented movies? Was it the Americans, the Brits, or the French? The answer is, a bit of all three. Cinema has been an international enterprise from the beginning.

THE WAGON DRIVER

The father of African cinema is Senegalese filmmaker Ousmane Sembène. He wrote and directed the 1963 film *Borom Sarret* (*The Wagon Driver*), which is believed to be **the first film made in Africa by a black African director**. Set in the capital city of Dakar, the movie shows a day in the life of a man trying to make a living driving a cart around the city. Senegal was a French colony at the time, and the **government had declared it illegal for Africans to make movies**. Sembène had to make the film secretly, with friends and family playing all the parts. He shot the 18-minute movie with a 16 mm camera on leftover film stock given to him by a friend who lived in Europe.

MARVEL GOES TO CHINA

Have you seen *Iron Man 3*? Unless you've been to Beijing (below) recently, chances are you haven't seen all of it.

In an attempt to guarantee the movie was a hit in that country, the filmmakers created **a special, China-only version** of the film. It has an extra subplot involving doctors at the hospital where Tony Stark gets an operation; one doctor is played by Fan Bingbing, one of China's biggest stars. Why go to all that trouble? Money, of course: China is expected to surpass the United States as the biggest movie-watching country in the world.

HOORAY FOR ALL THE "-WOOD"S

Hollywood will always be the place most associated with the movie business, but that doesn't mean it has no competition. In fact, **the world's most productive film industry isn't Hollywood at all, but Bollywood**, in India. India's capital city, Mumbai, used to be known as Bombay, and so when the moviemaking took off in that city, the nickname "Bollywood" was born. Bollywood releases more than 1,600 films per year—that's nearly four times as many as Hollywood.

Hollywood isn't even the world's second-busiest film industry—that honor goes to **Nollywood, in Nigeria**. Nigerians produce about 1,000 films per year, and the industry employs more Nigerians than any field except agriculture. Most Nigerian films are shot in a couple of weeks with budgets of around US$10,000. Many Nollywood films are made specifically for DVD sales rather than to be shown in cinemas.

Wait, there's more! How can we forget Chollywood (China), Dhaliwood (Bangladesh), Ghollywood (Ghana), Hallyuwood (South Korea), Kollywood (Nepal), Mollywood (Malaysia), Swahiliwood (Tanzania), Ugawood (Uganda), Wellywood (New Zealand), and Zollywood (Zimbabwe).

FILM FACTS

THE AUSTRALIAN FILM *The Story of the Ned Kelly Gang*, a silent film released in 1906, is considered to be the first full-length movie ever made.

THE 1995 BOLLYWOOD FILM *Dilwale Dulhaniya Le Jayenge* (The Big-Hearted Will Take Away the Bride) has been shown continuously in one Mumbai theater for more than 1,000 weeks.

THE CINEWORLD THEATER in Glasgow, Scotland, is the world's tallest movie theater—a 12-story building with 18 screens that can seat well over 4,000 audience members total.

THE BIGGEST CINEMA in terms of audience size is the Kinepolis Madrid, which boasts 25 screens and can seat more than 9,000 people.

Television

You might think you love TV. But China has by far the largest total number of televisions on Earth—more than 400 million sets!

DON'T GET CAUGHT

On the Russian show, *The Intercept*, a contestant was presented with a car that was immediately reported to Moscow police as stolen. If the contestant could avoid the cops for the duration of the show, he or she got to keep the car. **Apparently, authorities hoped the show would discourage car thieves.** But the too-popular-for-its-own-good show had the opposite effect, increasing car thefts instead! *The Intercept* was canceled after a single season.

BLACK AND WHITE

South Africa did not allow television broadcasts until 1976—much later than other African nations. Kenya, Sierra Leone, Congo, Rhodesia (now Zimbabwe), and Ethiopia are just a few of the African countries that had introduced TV in the 1960s, and Morocco and Nigeria already had it in the late 1950s.

South Africa's prime minister at the time compared television to the atomic bomb and claimed it had a corrupting influence on youth. **But it was the *liberalizing* influence the state actually feared.** One politician admitted that the introduction of television would mean "the destruction of white South Africa." We can't say whether TV brought about a more equal country. But apartheid, the country's system of state-enforced racial segregation, had been around for more than 30 years when TV arrived. Negotiations to end apartheid began just over a dozen years after TV's arrival.

COUCH POTATO CROSS-POLLINATION

International viewers love American crime shows, such as *CSI: Crime Scene Investigation* and its many spin-offs. Romanians are partial to *CSI: New York* and Hungarians go for *CSI: Miami*. Meanwhile, Italian viewers can't get enough of the naval versions, *NCIS* and *NCIS: Los Angeles*.

Some shows are subtitled in the local languages, but often the dialogue is translated and re-recorded. In the United Arab Emirates, *The Simpsons* is edited and re-recorded as *Al Shamshoon*. Homer is called Omar and Marge is Mona. Because alcohol is forbidden in Muslim countries, **Omar drinks soda instead of Duff beer,** and nobody visits Moe's bar at all! Sorry, Moe!

Other times it makes more sense to remake the show completely. Russian TV has aired their own remakes of many American comedies, like *It's Always Sunny in Moscow* and *Everybody Loves Kostya*. Iranians made their own version of *Modern Family* and called it *Haft Sang* (Seven Stones). And *Glee* was revamped for Chinese viewers, where it's called *My Youth High Eight Degrees*.

GOOD SHOW OR NOT GOOD SHOW?

If the name of the game is crazy competitions on TV, then Japan is definitely winning. The infamous game show *AKBINGO* puts its young female contestants through all sorts of miseries, such as being forced to come **face-to-face with massive lizards** while the ladies have juicy steaks attached to their foreheads. Contestants on *Dasshutsu Game DERO!* tried to solve puzzles while placed in extreme situations, such as **stuck in a room that was rapidly filling with water or sinking into a giant pile of sand**.

Theater

Whether it's a high-priced Broadway show, a song-and-dance number at an amusement park, or a magician working a street corner, it's all theater.

MARATHON PERFORMANCES

How long should a play be? Most of us figure we'll spend roughly two hours watching a live performance. But expectations are very different in different parts of the world. Here are a few examples.

- In Oberammergau, in southern Germany, every 10 years they perform what's called a "passion play" (a depiction of the crucifixion of Jesus Christ). The play **involves around 2,000 actors and takes the better part of a day** to perform.
- *Mahābhārata*, an epic tale about the war for control of ancient India, has been called the world's longest poem. When a French adaptation was staged in the 1980s, the running time was 11 hours.
- The Indonesian islands of Bali and Java are famous for their **lengthy, hypnotic performances** of *wayang kulit*, with **elaborate shadow puppets**, and *gambuh*, a highly stylized type of dance (below). Traditionally, these performances would go on for days without a break. Today, performances are trimmed to four or five hours, to suit the limited patience of tourists.

SHENG AND DAN

If you hear the word "opera," your first thought might be of a plus-sized lady wearing a horned helmet. But **China has its own rich opera tradition**. Chinese operas (above) are different from Western ones in many ways. For instance, Chinese operas have set characters that are immediately recognizable to the audience. *Sheng* is the male role, and there are various subcategories: *xiaosheng* is a young, handsome male character, *laosheng* is an older character with high status, and *wusheng* is a male warrior. Female characters are called *dan* (above), and they also come in specific types: *guimendan* is the young, flirtatious female character, *laodan* is an older woman, and *daomadan* is a female warrior. Traditionally, female characters in Chinese opera were portrayed by male actors.

NIGERIAN THEATER

Nigeria gained its independence from Great Britain in 1960, and in the years that followed, the West African country saw a blossoming of African-centric art forms (below), including theater. **A popular form called Yoruba opera uses folktales, mime, music, and dance to both celebrate and satirize Nigerian culture.** In addition to its traditional forms, Nigeria has also produced brilliant playwrights in the Western sense of the word. The best-known is Wole Soyinka, who became the first African to win the Nobel Prize for Literature in 1986.

BROADWAY FACTS

THE NICKNAME "GREAT WHITE WAY" dates back to 1880, when streetlights were first installed, and people were amazed by the way Broadway looked at night.

THE DESIGNATION "BROADWAY" isn't defined by location, but rather by the number of seats in the theater. All Broadway theaters have 500 seats or more.

MOST BROADWAY THEATERS don't have a row L, because the letter L can be too easily confused with the number 1. Theater managers didn't want audience members to think they had first-row seats when they didn't.

THE FIRST MUSICAL in the sense we define it today was *The Black Crook*, performed on Broadway in 1866.

THE LONGEST-RUNNING BROADWAY SHOW in history is The *Phantom of the Opera* (above), which has logged more than 12,000 performances.

Made by Hand

Arts and crafts walk a fine line between useful and beautiful. The best ones are both!

THE POWER OF SHADDA

The tradition of *shadda* (carpet) weaving has been an important part of Azerbaijani culture for thousands of years. Designs are made for specific life events, such as weddings and funerals, and the *shadda* are **imbued with particular meanings and powers**. For example, the Garda Klik *shadda kilim* (above) is woven for weddings; it's said to help protect the couple from bad luck and misfortune. The *chilla-shadda* is a red-and-blue patterned carpet that is woven to ward off bad events in the future. There's also a ritual where young women sit on the *chilla-shadda* and discuss their futures; the carpet is then left out for a week, exposed to the sky, in order to gather power and help the women's dreams come true.

BRINGING BACK KIFFA

In Mauritania, traditional kiffa beads served both as jewelry and as talismans that protected the wearer. Finely ground glass of various colors was mixed with spit (yes) and blades of grass were used to create intricate swirling patterns. Then the beads were baked over

hot coals. Kiffa beads come in a variety of shapes, including spheres, diamonds, and triangles. The colors are very important; blue beads represent heaven, for example, while white ones represent purity. Unfortunately, by the 1970s all the traditional bead makers had died out, and the skill was lost for a time. At the close of the 20th century, groups of Mauritanian women began working to relearn how to make the beads and bring back the art form.

GOODBYE, AÑO VIEJO

Around New Year's, people in rural Colombia make *año viejo* (old year) dolls (right). **These life-sized, stuffed dolls are dressed in old clothes**, and they're designed to represent something that the maker wants to leave behind in the past year. Sometimes people write messages on little signs for the dolls to carry. At midnight on New Year's Eve, the dolls are set on fire, so that whatever bad stuff you've packed into that doll will not follow you into the new year.

ART OR NUISANCE?

Street art has always been controversial. After all, one person's art is another person's graffiti.

One of the earliest "scratches" was a sort of advertisement carved into a paving stone in the ancient city of Ephesus in modern-day Turkey. Symbols for wine, women, and a foot suggested which direction to walk if you wanted to find the wine and the women.

Modern graffiti—or street art—has come a long way from scratches into paving stones.

- **Berlin, Germany (below):** From 1961 to 1989, the city was bisected by the Berlin Wall, which was a magnet for political graffiti (on the free, western side at least!). Now the wall is no more, and street art has spilled out all over the city.
- **Bogota, Colombia:** Street art had been around for a long time, but when police shot and killed an artist named Diego Felipe Becerra in 2011, it kicked off a protest art movement that has not slowed since.
- **Cape Town, South Africa:** Since the end of legal segregation in 1994, street art has flooded across Cape Town.

Zeros and Ones

Video games, apps, and other digital entertainment might not have the long history of theater or the rich cultural significance of handicrafts, but no matter where you go, people find them hard to resist.

IT'S A SMALL APOCALYPSE, AFTER ALL

A trade association called CableTV.com conducted a study of what video games are the most popular in various countries. These are the top three games, ranked by how many countries picked them as their favorite.

- The soccer game **FIFA 17 is the most popular video game in the world**—it tops the list in 15 different soccer-mad countries, including Bangladesh, Egypt, Ghana, Ireland, Nigeria, and Uruguay.
- Not far behind is a World War I–based game called **Battlefield 1**, which is the most popular video game in 13 countries, including Croatia, Norway, Sweden, and Turkey. It might seem weird that it's also the most popular game in Saudi Arabia! But the World War I era coincided with an event called the Arab Revolt, which led to the birth of Arab nationalism across the Middle East. So perhaps there is some nostalgia involved.
- The number 3 slot went to **Horizon Zero Dawn** in which a plucky female protagonist has to fight her way through a postapocalyptic landscape populated with killer dinosaur robots, because why not? The 10 countries devoted to this game include Australia, Germany, Japan, and South Africa.

GOTTA BAN 'EM ALL

In Saudi Arabia, all forms of Pokémon are banned for religious reasons.

Part of the problem stems from what the Saudi Arabians view as the **gambling-like nature of the Pokéverse**. And then there are those geometric symbols, which are features of both the cards and the digital versions. Some of the symbols, according to Saudi Arabia's top religious official, feature "six-pointed stars, a symbol of international Zionism and the state of Israel." And it doesn't stop there! Other symbols the authorities find distasteful include "crosses, sacred for Christians, triangles significant for Freemasons, and symbols of Japan's Shintoism." (Pokémon creators deny that their designs are religious in any way.)

SO, YOU THINK YOU CAN RAP?

China has a massively popular reality competition show, which works the same way as shows like *The Voice*. But instead of pop music, the show **The Rap of China is focused on hip-hop—or XiHa**, as it's known in China. The gist of the show will be very familiar to anyone who's ever watched a talent-competition. Each episode has a challenge (such as freestyling, or one-on-one rap battles), and contestants work with coaches to prepare their best performances. The least-successful person is eliminated at the end of the episode.

What makes *The Rap of China* unique is that it doesn't air on traditional television. Instead, the show can only be found online, hosted by a streaming service called iQiyi (essentially, Chinese Netflix). But just because it's an online-only show doesn't mean *The Rap of China* is in any way small-time. The budget for the first season was about 200 million yen (~US$30 million) and racked up 2.5 billion views.

SPRINGTIME FOR WOLFENSTEIN

Due to its painful history, for a long time Germany had an across-the-board ban on Nazi imagery of any kind. That included, for example, the Wolfenstein series, **World War II–focused games** in which Nazis are clearly the bad guys. In order to be sold in Germany at all, Wolfenstein had to be heavily edited. For example, the Adolf Hitler character in the German version of the game does not show the historical figure's iconic moustache.

In 2018, rules in Germany were loosened somewhat. Going forward, World War II games will be reviewed, and decisions will be made on a case-by-case basis. This brings imported games in line with the rules Germany applies to films.

Organized sports can be traced back to ancient Greece, which held festivals around what are sometimes called **"classical games."**

Early sports include **wrestling**, which is the only sport mentioned in the Bible, and soccer, which was invented in ancient China, where it was called *cuju*.

ПОЧТА СССР 1977
6к+3к

SPORTS AND GAMES

Things have changed a lot since organized sports were first invented in **ANCIENT GREECE.** Today there are sports and games and recreational activities to suit every taste—even if your taste involves battling your friends for **a headless goat** . . .

Namibia is one of the few African countries to have declared a national sport by law—in fact, they're so sports mad they've declared three of them! **Soccer, rugby, and netball are all national sports of Namibia.** Netball is somewhat like basketball, with raised hoops on either end of the court.

Everyone's Favorite

A national sport is a game that's central to a particular country's identity. Some countries are so serious about this that they enshrine their national sports in law.

THAT REALLY GETS MY GOAT

It's fitting that the grueling and perilous landscape of Central Asia should give rise to a grueling and perilous national sport. In Afghanistan it's called *buzkashi* (below), while Kyrgyzstan's national sport is similar but called *kok boru*. Both versions are a bit like polo except the horses run faster and a bit like hockey except the clashes are more violent. Oh, and instead of a ball or puck, the **players chase down a dead goat**.

Before a match, a goat is slaughtered, and its head and hooves removed. Then two teams on horseback battle to grab the goat off the ground—not a small feat because the carcass can weigh around 80 pounds (36 kg)—and then either toss it into a goal (in *kok boru*) or ride a specific circuit with the goat (in *buzkashi*). Other players, also on horseback, try to snatch the goat away. Falls, dislocated joints, and internal injuries are just a part of this hardcore goat-grabbing experience.

IT'S ONLY FUN WHEN SOMETHING BLOWS UP

At the end of a long day, many Colombians like to unwind with their national pastime: a friendly game of *tejo*. **Tejo is a throwing game that's a bit like horseshoes, but with an explosive twist.**

Players throw a rounded stone, the *tejo* (right), at a box filled with clay. Tucked into the clay is the target, or *bocin*, and whoever gets closest wins. But that's not the whole story—surrounding the *bocin* are little triangles called *mechas*, which are packed with gunpowder. When you hit a *mecha*, everybody knows it because it goes off like a loud firecracker. You actually get more points for hitting the *bocin* without setting off the *mecha* . . . but c'mon, what fun is that?

TAG, YOU'RE OUT

The national sport of Bangladesh is *kabaddi* (right); it's basically **a very intense, complex version of the kids' game, tag**. *Kabaddi* (also called *ha-du-du* in Bangladesh) is played with two teams on a rectangular court. One person, called the raider, attempts to tag as many of the other team as he (or she) can and get back to his own side of the court before getting tackled by the other team. This all happens in the timespan of one breath; the raider must chant, "*Kabaddi*" over and over as he runs, to prove he's not breathing in any extra air.

Kabbadi was originally an Indian invention and remains popular there. Other countries, including Pakistan, Iran, Malaysia, Japan, South Korea, Thailand, and the United Kingdom, also have teams. In South Asia, *kabbadi* tournaments are aired on television with all the trappings you'd expect from professional sports, like corporate sponsorships and excited commentary from experts.

TAKE ME OUT TO THE OINĂ

Some sports become "national pastimes" because people are obsessed with them, but in the case of Romania, a game called *oină* was declared the national sport in an attempt to save it. *Oină* (below) is a stickball game that dates back to the 1300s, and the Romanian government became concerned that young kids were no longer playing it; so, *oină* was declared the country's "national sport" in 2014. *Oină* is somewhat like baseball, with two teams of 11 players who take turns at bat. In fact, some claim that baseball has its roots in *oină*, played by Romanian immigrants to the United States. Fans of America's "inventor of baseball" Abner Doubleday would dispute this, but that's what they say in Bucharest!

Traditional Sports

Professional sports rely on the latest innovations to improve performance, be it new uniforms or high-tech gear. Some traditional sports, on the other hand, date back hundreds of years and have never changed at all—and most think they never need to!

HORSE WRESTLING

Er Enish (right) is a type of wrestling developed by the nomadic horsemen of the Kyrgyz Republic. It's pretty simple to play, although not necessarily easy to win. Two competitors on horseback face off in an arena, and the man who can pull his opponent off his horse first is the winner.

AMAZING RACE

Every year, racing fans converge on the Indian state of Kerala to watch the Vallam Kali, better known as the snake boat races (below). The boats are traditional war canoes that come in two sizes—one with 64 rowers and the other with an amazing 128 people all rowing in sync. The snake boats are still made with the same basic design and techniques as the originals were, more than 650 years ago. There are a number of different snake boat racing events in Kerala; the most famous is probably the Nehru Cup, which has been held on Punnamada Lake every year since 1954.

LOG THROWING

The amazing caber toss (right) is inextricably linked with the Scottish highlands. A caber is a long, narrow log that's roughly 17 feet (5 m) long and weighs around 150 pounds (68 kg). There is no officially required length or weight, but the point is, a caber is big—it's at least the size of you and two friends standing on top of one another.

In a caber toss, a competitor lifts up the log so that it points at the sky and then throws it so that the log flies end over end and lands pointing straight ahead. The throw is scored by judges, who base their marks on the accuracy of the throw. Points are not awarded for the quality of kilt the thrower is wearing—but he'd better have one because it's Scotland, mate!

DIVING FOR YAMS

The Republic of Vanuatu is made up of about 80 islands that can be found east of Australia and just north of New Zealand. The people of the island of Pentecost practice a death-defying ritual called land diving (left), in which participants leap off a 98-foot structure with nothing but a vine tied to their ankles. Though many have asked, no outsiders are allowed to participate. That's how land diving became the inspiration for bungee jumping! But land diving is not a wacky "extreme sport" in Vanuatu—it's a revered annual tradition that celebrates the yam harvest.

SPORTS FACTS

CAMEL RACING is popular across the Middle East, as well as in Mongolia and Australia. Well-trained camels can run at about 40 miles per hour (65 kph) for short sprints. In Persian Gulf countries like Oman and Qatar, children are often forced to work as jockeys because they are lighter than adults.

A SPORT CALLED "EXTREME IRONING" began in England in the 1980s. Participants try to outdo one another by ironing clothes in the most outrageous places—in the middle of a busy highway, atop a waterfall, while kayaking, and even under water.

MUAY THAI (THAI BOXING) is sometimes called "the art of eight limbs" because, in addition to using their fists, Thai boxers (below) also use both feet, elbows, and shins to strike their opponents.

Simply the Best

Most of us would love to be the champion of something. . . . But you won't believe the strange ways some people like to compete!

DON'T GET BOGGED DOWN

A bog is a type of wetland, composed primarily of rainwater, mud, and peat (the mucky remains of decomposed plants). If a bog is wet enough, you can kind of, more or less, swim through it. But of course, nobody would ever intentionally do that . . . right?

Wrong. **The World Bog Snorkeling championships** are held annually in Llanwrtyd Wells, Wales. Swimmers compete for the best time across two lengths of a 60-yard (55 m) peat bog. Llanwrtyd Wells also hosts a bog-snorkeling triathlon (running followed by some snorkeling followed by a mountain-bike ride through the bog). There are also bog-snorkeling events in Ireland, Australia, and Sweden.

POLE SCRUM

Bo-taoshi (below right) is a madcap game played by cadets at Japan's National Defense Academy. **It's a bit like capture the flag if capture the flag involved players standing on one another's heads.**

In *bo-taoshi*, each team of roughly 150 players has to hold up a tall pole; the first team to bring down the other side's pole wins. Half the players on each team hold and guard their own pole, while the other half "attack" the pole of the opposing team. Once the match gets going, the result is two **mosh pits of people climbing over one another**—even vaulting over each other's backs!—to try and get control of the other team's pole and drag it down to the ground.

AT THE ROACH RACES

One night, at the bar of the Story Bridge Hotel in Brisbane, Australia, two men got into an argument. That's probably not an unusual event, let's be honest. But on this night in 1982, the argument sparked a new type of competition. The men were debating who had the fastest cockroaches in his neighborhood, and they decided to settle the matter with a roach race in the parking lot. So began a tradition that has blossomed into the World Championship Cockroach Races, held every Australia Day for almost 40 years. **Humans can bring their "athletes" from home or purchase them from the bar.** For that brief, shining moment, one of the world's most-hated pests is the star of the show.

ROWDY RODDY CAMEL

From sumo in Japan to the antics of the WWF, people everywhere love wrestling. But nothing quite matches the Turkish version: rather than man versus man, it's camel versus camel.

Camel wrestling (below) only happens during mating season, when males are far more aggressive than they are the rest of the year. An annual camel-wrestling festival takes place over the course of three months in Selcuk, Turkey, drawing some 20,000 visitors. Camels square off two at a time, tripping and pushing one another until one gives up. The winner goes on to wrestle the next competitor until a champion is crowned. Animal-rights activists complain about the exploitation, but after nearly 2,500 years, the practice is unlikely to go away any time soon.

Ain't We Got Fun?

What some people do for fun may surprise or even alarm you. On the other hand, maybe you'd like to join in! If so, put these strange recreational activities on your bucket list.

HERE'S MUD IN YOUR EYE

It might not be the world's weirdest hobby, but it's surely in the top ten: *hikaru dorodango*, the Japanese art of **polished mud balls** (right). Practitioners of this highly meditative form of sculpting take handfuls of mud and smooth them, over and over again for a *very* long time, until the final result looks as shiny as a billiard ball. No doubt you're currently picturing mud as brown, but it needn't be. Different ingredients and types of soil can result in *dorodango* in every color of the rainbow.

CAGE OF DEATH

If you think petting zoos are for babies and swimming with dolphins is dull, perhaps you should head out to Darwin, in Australia's Northern Territory. At an aquarium and reptile house called Crocosaurus Cove, you'll find the **Cage of Death**—the continent's only "crocodile dive."

Visitors climb into a clear box, which is then lowered into the saltwater crocodile enclosure. Keepers feed the crocs while you're with them, making sure they're nice and lively while you're mere inches of plastic away from one of the animal kingdom's most vicious killers.

NICE FOOD IF YOU CAN CARVE IT

Visitors to state fairs in America's agricultural regions are surely familiar with the power and the glory of the butter sculpture (right). **The Iowa State Fair's traditional butter cow sculpture, for example, is nearly six feet high (1.8 m) and weighs around 600 pounds (272 kg).**

Butter sculpture dates back to the Renaissance in northern Europe. In 1536 a famous chef named Bartolomeo Scappi carved a nine-course meal for Pope Pius V that portrayed mythological scenes like Hercules fighting the Nemean Lion. Dessert was the Roman goddess Diana made from spun sugar.

HIP HOP– LITERALLY

Swedes invented *Kaninhop* in the 1970s. *Kaninhop* takes the grandeur of showjumping for horses and shrinks it down . . . way down . . . to bunny size. The first national **bunny-jumping championship** was held in Sweden in 1987, and before long, other Nordic countries hopped in, too. Today, rabbit hopping associations and competitions exist across Europe, North America, and Australia.

There are five levels of competition, depending on how high a bar the rabbits can clear, from mini (7.9 in; 20 cm) to elite (19.7 in; 50 cm). There are also rabbit agility events where bunnies navigate obstacles, such as tire jumps and seesaws. And if you're sarcastically wondering, "But what about guinea pigs," the answer is yes, guinea pig agility contests are a thing, too.

Amazing Feats

Whether it's one person doing something amazing or thousands of people doing something simultaneously, the wild world of sports has seen some incredible achievements.

STRONG AS A MOUNTAIN

How strong are you? Probably not as strong as Icelandic strongman Hafþór Júlíus Björnsson (left). In 2015, he set a world record by taking five steps while carrying a log on his back. Doesn't sound like much? **The log weighed 1,430 pounds (650 kg), and it took 50 people to move the log after Björnsson was done.** In those five steps, he'd broken a record that had stood for about 1,000 years, from the time of the Vikings. But Björnsson may be most famous for his appearances on the TV show *Game of Thrones*, where he played a character called, appropriately enough, the Mountain.

TAKE A SHOT

One factor that helped make basketball as popular as it is today is the shot clock. Introduced in the 1950s, **the shot clock keeps the game lively** by forcing teams to keep the ball moving toward the net at all times. That urgency can make for some high-scoring games, even at amateur levels. For example, at a Swedish high school basketball tournament in 1974, **13-year-old Mats Wermelin scored an astounding 272 points in one game.**

The first female player to break the 100-point barrier at the high school level was Iowa's Denise Long, who scored 111 points in one game in 1968. Long went on to be the first woman drafted by the National Basketball Association; she was drafted by the San Francisco Warriors in 1969. On the professional side, Wilt Chamberlain scored a 100-point game against the NY Knicks in 1962.

RUNNING FROM JAGUARS

To some athletes, there's nothing worth doing that isn't worth taking to extremes. Why run a boring old marathon when you can run an **ultramarathon**?

Defined as any race longer than the traditional marathon, ultramarathons frequently take place over not just long distances but in extreme environments. **The Marathon des Sables, for instance, covers 217 miles (350 km) of desert territory in Morocco.** The Jungle Ultra begins in Peru's Cloud Forest, some 10,000 feet (3,000 m) above sea level; from there, runners must navigate 143 miles (230 km) of jungle, mountains, and rivers, and (ideally) not get attacked by the jaguars native to the area.

IT'S A GLORIOUS COUNTRY?

When it comes to group organization, few activities can compete with Pyongyang, North Korea's sports event (of a sort) called Glorious Country. Glorious Country is a mass-gymnastics event involving **synchronized performances of more than 100,000 people**. The event is held in May Day Stadium on Rungrada Island in the middle of Pyongyang; May Day Stadium is said to be the largest sports and recreation venue in the world.

The highlight of every event is billed as "the largest picture in the world," where thousands of participants all hold up pictures at the same time to create a single image. Performers are selected at around age five; once chosen, they are trained to perform in the "games" for years, usually with no idea how long their tenure will last.

Games People Play

No matter how old we get, we all need to play from time to time.

HOP ACROSS THE WORLD

On schoolyards, sidewalks, and driveways all over the world, **kids play a game that involves tossing a stone and then jumping across a grid to fetch it**. In India the game is known as *stapu* or *paandi*, while Syrian kids play *hajla* and Iranians call it *laylay*. In Brazil it's called *amarelinha*, in Mexico it's *bebeleche* and in Cuba it's *el pon*. It's called *sabancchigi* in South Korea and *piko* in the Philippines. In Albania it's *rrasavi* and in Romania it's *șotron*. The design of the courts changes from place to place, and there may be specific rules that are different. But nothing unites the world like hopscotch.

CAUGHT THE DRAGON BY THE TAIL

A fun playground game from China is called **1,2,3 Dragon, Catch the Dragon,** or something similar. It's a pretty straightforward game to play. All the kids stand in a line with their hands on each other's shoulders. The kid in the front is the dragon's head, and the kid in back is the tail. The game involves the dragon's head running to grab the tail. But it's not quite that simple because the dragon's body needs to stay connected the entire time. It's a conga line and tag in one!

ROOSTER FIGHT!

The Brazilian kids' game called *luta de galo* (fight of the roosters) is as much fun to watch as it is to play—arguably more fun, depending on how you feel about hopping. You'll need two players, each with a handkerchief or some piece of cloth in their back pockets. To play, you cross your right arm over your chest to prevent you from using it. Using your left hand, you try to snatch the other person's handkerchief before he or she gets yours. Seems simple enough, right? Oh, we forgot to mention . . . **you have to hop on one foot the entire time**. If you put your foot down, you lose. So, get ready and, as they say in Portuguese, *um, dois, três . . . lutam!*

CITIZENS OF SKATEISTAN

When an Australian named Oliver Percovich visited his girlfriend in Kabul, Afghanistan, where she was working at the time, he brought his skateboard with him. The kids he met around town were fascinated with Percovich's board and wanted to learn how to skate, too. Even (maybe especially) girls were eager to get their own boards. This led Percovich to found Skateistan, a **nonprofit organization that promotes skateboarding** as a vehicle for community-building and education. Skateboarding is now the most popular sport for girls in all of Afghanistan!

Just Plain Fun

Sure, outdoor sports are fine for some people, but some of us prefer our competition around the table.

MANCALA EVERYWHERE

One classic genre of games is "pit and pebble," or *mancala*. **The name *mancala* comes from an Arabic word that means "to move" or "to transfer."** *Mancala* games are all played on a carved wooden board (right). Two players take turns moving the stones around the board; usually the goal is to capture all of your opponents' stones. It's a game that's played all over the world—from Ghana and Uganda to the Philippines, Oman, and India—albeit with variations in rules.

CHESS + POOL = CARROM

Carrom (right) is a popular tabletop game that originated in Southeast Asia but has spread across the world. The game combines some elements of chess (you play with a number of pawns and one queen) with elements of pool or snooker (the goal is to get pieces into corner "pockets"). It's so popular that there are tournaments and even professional *carrom* players. The International Carrom Federation, founded in 1988, has its headquarters in the Maldives. Member countries include India, Pakistan, Malaysia, Sri Lanka, Korea, Japan, Germany, Switzerland, Czech Republic, Poland, France, United Kingdom, and the United States.

CHECKERS IN AFRICA

Liberians play a traditional board game called *queah*, which is named for the Queah tribe who invented it. It's somewhat like checkers (right), except the playing area is smaller and made of interconnected diamonds rather than straight squares. The goal, as in checkers, is to **move your pieces across the board and capture the other player's pieces by leaping over them**. There are a number of other checkers-like games in West Africa, including *yoté* and *choko*. They all have the same goal—moving pieces to try and capture the pieces of your opponent.

READY SET GO!

The oldest board game that people still play regularly today is probably *weiqi*, known to us today as Go (right). **The game was invented in China well over 2,000 years ago.** Two players, one with white stones and one with black, place their pieces on a 19- by 19-inch (48 × 48 cm) grid. The goal of the game is to take control of the board by taking your opponent's pieces "prisoner." Although Go is most popular in Asia, the International Go Federation has 75 member countries, which reflects the worldwide popularity of the game. The second Latin American Go Congress, for example, was held in October 2018 in the city of Antigua, Guatemala.

TRANSPORTATION AND COMMUNICATION

You may not sense it, but **our world has been gradually shrinking for a long time.** These days, people think nothing of having dinner in New York followed by breakfast in London the next morning. Digital communication has also made the world feel smaller and more connected than ever before.

In ancient Greece, when a soldier named Pheidippides wanted to tell his Athenian friends that their side had won a battle against the Persian Army, the soldier had to run the 26.2 miles from the battlefield in Marathon, which is where the word **"marathon"** comes from.

Back when Christopher Columbus (right) sailed the ocean blue, his journey across the Atlantic took over two months.

More than **70 million** cars are made in the world every year.

Getting Around

Our first—and to this day, most reliable—form of transportation is our own feet. But ever since horses were domesticated in 4000 BCE, we've been looking for better, faster, and sometimes weirder ways to get from here to there.

HIP-HOPPING ON THE MATATU

What is part radio station, part rolling art museum, and part death trap? It's the *matatu* minibuses of Nairobi, Kenya (right).

Matatus are city buses that are painted in colorful, graffiti-like styles. They're as elaborately decorated as they are poorly regulated. Famous for ignoring traffic laws and laughing in the face of safety, *matatu* drivers are the bane of more sober-minded motorists. They frequently play loud music to attract customers, some of whom hop on and hang off the side of the bus rather than sitting down. City officials have tried to regulate, and even ban, *matatus* but with little success. Young people of Nairobi especially love the *matatu*'s music-blaring, mad-driving, bone-rattling ways.

YOU BRING TWO FRIENDS, AND THEY BRING TWO FRIENDS, AND . . .

On the island of Mindanao, in the Philippines, there's a very friendly method of transportation called the *habal-habal* (right). *Habal-habals* are motorcycles that have boards attached to each side so that many people can ride at the same time. They are popular in Mindanao because so many of the roads aren't passable by car—only two-wheeled vehicles can get through. People use *habal-habals* to get around, to transport goods to market, and even, in a pinch, as emergency ambulances.

Habal-habals are illegal in the Philippines because they aren't particularly safe. Balance is essential, and if the driver loses control of the bike, there's nothing to protect the passengers from serious injury. But the fact that *habal-habals* are illegal hasn't reduced the popularity of this nimble two-wheeled vehicle that has room for you, your friends, and even your friends' chickens.

ACROPHOBICS NEED NOT APPLY

If you decide to go zip-lining (above) in Costa Rica, best leave your acrophobia—or fear of heights—at home. Jungle zip-lining first started in the 1990s, when scientists used it as a way to study the upper canopies of Costa Rica's numerous rainforests. These days, there are canopy tours all over the country. Tourists can zip their way over the Monkey Jungle of Tamarindo, the Montezuma Waterfall, and even the Arenal Volcano! But be sure to bring your sensible shoes—flip-flops are strictly forbidden on zip lines.

CUCKOO FOR COCO TAXI

New York has yellow cabs and London has black ones, but Cuba has . . . coconuts?

A Coco Taxi (below) is a gas-powered scooter that has three seats in the back and a big shell around it, making the vehicle look vaguely like a coconut.

Coco Taxis were first seen on the streets of Havana in the 1990s, serving the city's growing tourist population. These days, there are actually two flavors of Coco Taxi—bright yellow ones are only for foreign visitors; dark blue Coco Taxis only serve Cubans.

CAR FACTS

THE COUNTRY WITH THE LARGEST NUMBER OF CARS OVERALL IS CHINA. But the country with the largest number of cars per person is the tiny nation of San Marino, which has more than 1,260 cars for every 1,000 people.

TIED FOR FEWEST CARS per capita are the nation of Togo and the islands of São Tomé and Príncipe, off the west coast of Africa; they have only 2 cars per 1,000 residents.

THREE-WHEELED CARS, sometimes called "auto rickshaws," are important forms of transportation in India and other countries.

Roads, Rails, and Bridges

If you're going to get there, you need a way to do it!

BOLIVIA'S ROAD OF DEATH

According to the Inter-Development Bank, Bolivia's North Yungas Road (right) is **the most dangerous road in the world**. The "Death Road," as it's sometimes called, clings to the side of a 2,000-foot (610 m) cliff. It has only one lane, no guardrails, and is often shrouded in fog. Between 200 and 300 people die on the road every year—mostly when their car or bus slides off the edge of the cliff into the rainforest ravine below. It's enough to make you ask yourself, "Do I really want to go to La Paz?"

MAGNET MAGIC?

When *Black Panther* filmmakers created Wakanda's vibranium-powered train system, they were inspired by a real-life system called maglev (below). Maglev is short for magnetic levitation, and while that may sound like magic, it's pure science. The power of magnets means that maglev trains don't need wheels or other moving parts; instead, they float above the track, with no friction to slow them down.

In 2016, **an experimental maglev train in Japan set a speed record of 374 miles per hour (603 kph)**. That works out to roughly one mile in ten seconds! You won't be able to actually ride that train until about 2027, though. The fastest currently operating maglev train is in Shanghai, China; it can take passengers from the airport to downtown at up to 268 miles per hour (431 kph).

BRIDGE TO OBLIVION

Norway is a country of many waterways and, as a result, a large number of bridges. None can compare to the Storseisundet (right), which connects the mainland to Averøya island. In most ways, Storseisundet is a normal bridge; it's about 850 feet (260 m) long and about 75 feet (23 m) high— no big deal. But the drive up to the bridge is anything but normal. Because motorists approach the bridge at such an extreme angle, it appears that about halfway across, the bridge drops off

into nothingness. It's just an optical illusion, but quite an unsettling one. Locally, Storseisundet is known as "the drunken bridge" because of its twisty nature, but you have to wonder if Norwegians are actually describing the state of mind of the architect who designed it.

DON'T MESS UP

Guoliang is a small village in the Taihang Mountains of China's Henan Province. Largely cut off from the rest of the province, for years the people of Guoliang asked the government for some sort of road. Help never arrived, and so in the 1970s, **Guloiang residents took charge themselves**. Using only hand tools, they dug a tunnel straight through the cliffs near their village (below). There were no trained engineers involved, just very hard-working amateurs, some of whom were killed during construction.

Today the tunnel road provides an amazing, if wildly dangerous, view of the Taihang mountains, thanks to the many "windows" that the residents carved into the side of the tunnel. But it's vital to drive very slowly on this twisty, single-lane road. Its **Chinese name translates as "the road that tolerates no mistakes."**

You Can't Get There from Here

No matter how fast we travel these days, there are still far-flung locales that remain almost—but not quite!—inaccessible to the modern world.

YOUR FLIGHT'S BEEN CANCELED

The Siberian village of Oymyakon (right) has been nicknamed "the coldest town on Earth" because subzero temperatures there are a way of life. With regular temperatures below minus 20 degrees Fahrenheit (−29°C), most houses don't have running water because there's no way to keep it from freezing in the pipes.

Ideally, people fly in and out of this part of the world, but **when the weather is quite bad, planes literally do not work: jet fuel freezes at about minus 40 degrees Fahrenheit (−40°C).** In that case, the only way in and out of Oymayakon is a two-day drive. Just be sure you bring enough gas—if your car is turned off for even a few minutes, the battery can freeze, and then you are in some serious trouble!

STAMP ME, PLEASE

Rapa Nui, better known to English speakers as Easter Island (below), is considered to be **one of the most isolated places in the world.** Unless you are a skilled sailor, the only way you'll get there is to fly from Chile. As a result, your passport will only say that you went as far as the west coast of South America—there'll be no mark proving you traveled all the way to French Polynesia. Unless, of course, you visit Easter Island's post office, on the corner of Atamu Tekena (Main Street) and Te Pito o Te Henua (The Street Below the Church). The postmaster will be happy to give your passport an official Rapa Nui stamp. The design features the massive stone Moai, which you might have heard called "Easter Island statues."

IT'S THE BOMB

Surely the most remote of Earth's seven continents is Antarctica—especially the research center called McMurdo (right), which is on the south part of Ross Island. Visitors have to arrive on military planes that are equipped with skis to be able to land on ice. In the middle of all the ice and snow sits a volcano, Mount Erebus, which creates its own lava lake that is 1,700 degrees Fahrenheit (927°C). From time to time, Mount Erebus releases "lava bombs"—chunks of molten rock that fly into the air and sometimes explode.

Antarctica has no permanent residents. In the warmer months, about 4,000 scientists live and work on Antarctica; the population drops to around 1,000 during the winter. There have been a few babies born on Antarctica; they are deemed residents of whatever country their parents are from.

The continent is governed under the 1959 Antarctic Treaty, stating that the region belongs to everyone (and, consequently, no one). It restricts activity on the continent to peaceful research only. No weapons are allowed on Antarctica, unless you count the lava bombs.

THE HIDDEN LOTUS

Motuo County (below) is in southeastern Tibet; the name means "hidden lotus" and for good reason. For a very long time, the only way to reach Motuo was to hike through the Himalayas. **There was no road, leaving the residents completely isolated from the rest of the region.** In the 1990s, the Chinese government finally built Bome–Medog Highway in the hopes of bringing the modern world to Motuo. The highway lasted precisely three days before being destroyed in a massive mudslide. It wasn't until October 2013 that a new road was finally completed.

The Ways of Water

Let the current carry you along these water-travel facts.

THE BIG ONES

The world's largest ships are the supertankers that carry oil and natural gas. Built in 1979, the supertanker *Knock Nevis* was in use until 2009. Over the years, it's been called the *Seawise Giant*, the *Happy Giant*, and the *Jahre Viking*, depending on who owned it at the time. *The Knock Nevis* wasn't just the largest ship ever built, it was the largest moving manmade object ever built.

When it comes to ships that carry people, the Royal Caribbean's three cruise ships—*Oasis of the Seas*, *Allure of the Seas*, and *Harmony of the Seas*—are the biggest. These massive floating cities can house more than 6,000 passengers, plus more than 2,000 crew members.

A MOST RELAXING TRIP

Boats have been around for so long, it's easy to imagine everything has been thought of. But then along comes the Norwegian inventor and sculptor Frank de Bruijn with his new invention, the Hot Tug (right)—**a sailable hot tub!** The floating hot tub seats eight, keeping the inside water at a relaxing 100 degrees Fahrenheit (38°C) while a small outboard motor pushes the wooden Hot Tug through far colder waters outside. Clearly, de Bruijn likes to spend as much time near water as he can—even his workshop sits on a barge in the port city of Rotterdam, the Netherlands.

THE SHIPBREAKERS

Global shipping depends on massive, steel-hulled ships that carry cargo all over the world. The ships last for decades, but eventually their steel hulls do wear out. When that happens, most of the retired ships end up on the shores of India, Bangladesh (right), and China. The ships are run aground on the beaches, where they are taken apart by tens of thousands of low-paid workers called "shipbreakers." Armed with blowtorches and minimal protective gear, shipbreakers slowly but surely disassemble the ships for scrap. One Bangladeshi man told a reporter that the beach used to be a tourist attraction. People would go **"watch men tear apart ships with their bare hands."** But ship deconstruction is extremely dangerous, and workers are killed on a regular basis. These days, the companies in charge try very hard to keep viewers away.

BASKET BOATS

Because of its amazing natural beauty, the state of Kerala in India is often called "God's Own Country." **Life in Kerala often centers on bodies of water—from beaches to canals to rice paddies.** In fact, people in Kerala don't just live "around" the water, many live on it. Kerala is famous for its houseboats, called *kettuvallam* (below). The *kettuvallam* have to share Kerala's waters with passenger boats (or "boat-buses") that help people get from place to place.

Traditional *kettuvallam* are made from wood held together with knotted ropes instead of nails. Their rounded, thatched roofs have inspired the nickname "basket boats." Most have a couple of bedrooms, a kitchen, a living area, and a toilet—although luxury *kettuvallams* can be much bigger.

Rules of the Road

When you have a whole bunch of people driving vehicles at high speeds, it's pretty important that everyone agrees on what the rules are. But some traffic laws may surprise you.

RIGHT OR LEFT?

In about two-thirds of the world's countries, cars drive on the right side of the road; the rest drive on the left. **The left-side preference comes from a British tradition of riding your horse on the left-hand side of a path.** That kept the rider's right hand free for waving or, in an emergency, drawing a sword. Most of these left-driving countries are former or current British territories.

SLIP SLIDING AWAY

Because the island of Guam has no natural source of sand, roads are made of ground-up coral held together by oil (below). That's fine . . . until it rains, and **the roads turn into a slick mess**. The speed limit on most roads in Guam, not surprisingly, is 35 miles per hour (56 kph).

DIRTY CAR YOU'VE GOT THERE, SHAME IF SOMETHING HAPPENED TO IT . . .

When people talk about strange driving laws, one that often comes up is that in Russia it's illegal to drive a dirty car (left). But the reality is more complicated.

True, **it is illegal to drive a car with a dirty license plate**, but that's true in many countries. What appears to be happening in Russia is that some unethical police officers are taking advantage of motorists. They claim the cars are "illegally dirty" and fine people on the spot or demand a bribe to look the other way.

DON'T, JUST DON'T, WE MEAN IT

Most countries have laws that relate to alcohol and driving. But Japan's rules may be the strictest. Not only is it illegal to drive while intoxicated, but even a sober passenger in a car with an intoxicated driver can be subjected to a high fine. That's tough but logical: if there's a drunk driver at the wheel, it's a bad idea to get in the car.

Special Delivery

The ancient Romans had the first postal service, called *cursus publicus*; it took around two months to get a message from Rome to Alexandria, Egypt. It's fair to say speeds have picked up quite a bit since then!

SMALL COUNTRY, BIG BUSINESS

Japan's mail system is far from the world's largest, but nevertheless, Japan Post is the largest financial institution in the world. This is because, in addition to delivering mail, **Japan Post (right) is also a bank and an insurance company.** In fact, when Japan Post was listed on the Tokyo Stock Exchange in 2015, it was valued at US$12 billion! That's a lot of stamps.

DEAR GOD . . .

Every year, about a thousand or so letters are sent to the Almighty via the nation of Israel. It makes sense: Israel is home to many of the holiest sites in Christianity, Judaism, and Islam. Where else would God pick up mail?

The head of the **Letters to God Department** (not a joke—that's what it's called) told a reporter that most of the letters are extremely personal. "We received a letter from a man who wrote to God after his wife passed away. He asked God to send his wife back to him in his dreams so he could see her once again. He missed her very much." Every year, the letters are blessed and put into cracks in Jerusalem's Western Wall (below).

OUTTA THIS WORLD

When you put a stamp on a letter and mail it, **you're sending the stamp on a little adventure**. But occasionally a stamp gets to go on a *huge* adventure. The furthest distance ever traveled by a postage stamp was 3,262,723,132 miles (5,250,843,896 km) in 2015. The stamp itself was issued in 1991 and had an illustration of Pluto (above left). Appropriate, then, that the stamp was aboard the *New Horizons* spacecraft (above right) in July 2015, when it flew past Pluto. *New Horizons* is still traveling outward toward a region of space called the Kuiper belt. It's the fifth craft ever to leave our solar system . . . and the only one, so far as we know, with appropriate postage.

YOU CAN'T SHOP THERE FROM HERE

Some companies refuse to ship to New Zealand because of the distance and expense. But the New Zealand Post found a way around this problem—it's called YouShop. New Zealanders who sign up with YouShop are given postal addresses in either the United Kingdom (for European shopping) or the United States (for North American shopping). The YouShop service collects the packages at those addresses and then ships them the rest of the way to the user's true address in New Zealand. Users do still have to pay the shipping costs, which can be substantial.

Can You Hear Me Now?

These days it seems that everyone in the world has something to say and phones to help them say it.

AFRICA CALLING

Cell phones have changed how people live all over the world but perhaps nowhere so much as in Africa. Take Nigeria: in the early 2000s, there were roughly 100,000 landlines in the whole country. These days, **Nigerians own more than 100 million cell phones**. A similar transformation is occurring in South Africa, Kenya, Rwanda, and many other countries.

Cell phones are increasingly used to pay bills (via electronic money). Farmers use them to exchange information about weather, and to find out where they can get the best prices for their crops. Teachers are using them in class because in many African countries it's far easier to get on the Internet with a smartphone than with a computer. People in refugee camps are also using cell phones to try and reconnect with family members. Rwandan president Paul Kagame said, "In 10 short years, what was once an object of luxury and privilege, the mobile phone, has become a basic necessity in Africa."

DON'T DROP IT IN THE TOILET

The world's most expensive phone is an iPhone 5 designed by Stuart Hughes. Made of 24-karat gold and decorated with 600 white diamonds and a rare black diamond for the home button, **the phone was sold to an anonymous Chinese billionaire for $15.3 million**.

NO SNEAKY PHOTOS!

It's not surprising that technology-obsessed Japan would be a leader in cell phones, known there as *keitai*. What might surprise you is that smartphones were fairly slow to catch on. **It wasn't until around 2016 that large numbers of people started using smartphones instead of flip phones (right).**

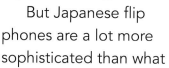

But Japanese flip phones are a lot more sophisticated than what you might be picturing. They can be used to play games, take photos, watch videos, and make purchases. Most Japanese cell phones are waterproof, and it's common for people to take them into the shower or bathtub! The government also requires that all phones must make a shutter sound when taking a picture—this rule is meant to combat *tousatsu*, or "sneak photography."

WILL YOU PLEASE HOLD?

"On-hold music"—the peppy-but-boring tunes that companies play while customers wait for someone to help them—was invented by the American Alfred Levy in the early 1960s. The phone line at his company had a loose wire, and that wire happened to touch a steel girder, which resulted in music from a nearby radio station being transmitted into the company phones. Levy decided it was much nicer to have something to listen to while he was waiting for a call to go through.

PHONE FACTS

MORE PEOPLE in the world own cell phones than own flush toilets.

CHINA has the largest number of smartphone users in the world— more than 782 million of them.

IN THE UNITED KINGDOM, 82 percent of people have smartphones—the highest percentage of any country.

THE FEAR OF SUDDENLY BEING UNABLE TO USE YOUR PHONE IS CALLED "NOMOPHOBIA"—"nomo" is short for "no mobile phone." But psychologists say nomophobia is really a sign of an anxiety disorder rather than a true, stand-alone phobia.

CELL-PHONE COLLECTOR Stefan Polgari lives in Dobsina, Slovakia, where he keeps about 3,500 vintage phones in a private "museum" in two rooms of his home.

Find Out More Fun Facts!

It's one big, beautiful, bizarre world out there, and this book can only scratch the surface of all there is to learn. If you like facts, there are a lot more to be found.

BOOKS

Almanacs are a type of reference book published every year; they're packed with current facts, statistics, and all kinds of information you didn't know you needed. Atlases are also crowded with facts, but they're focused on where things are—some atlases have tons of maps, while others only have a few, but they are still focused on geography. Annually updated record books like the one from Guinness will tell you who is the greatest and fastest and oldest and biggest. Here are a few titles that could help quench your thirst for facts.

Atlas Obscura. New York: Workman Publishing, 2016.

Guinness World Records. New York: Macmillan, annual.

National Geographic Almanac: Hot New Science. Washington, DC: National Geographic Partners, annual.

National Geographic Kids Almanac. Washington DC: National Geographic Partners, annual.

Now I Know! The Revealing Stories Behind the World's Most Interesting Facts. Avon, MA: Adams Media, 2013.

The Old Farmer's Almanac. Dublin, NH: Yankee Publishing, annual.

Ripley's Believe It Or Not! New York: Simon & Schuster, annual. London: Random House, annual.

The Way Things Work Now. New York: Houghton Mifflin, 2016.

The World Almanac and Book of Facts. New York: World Almanac Books, annual.

ONLINE

Those are some awesome books listed on the facing page, but let's not kid ourselves: if you're looking for a quick fact, you are probably going to go online to get it. One place to start that you may not have thought about is the website of your local library. Most libraries subscribe to online reference material that you can access for free as long as you have a library card.

And then, of course, there is the rest of the Internet. Just please be careful. There are a near-infinite number of "click-bait" pages that claim to offer "20 Facts About Something Crazy" that are poorly researched, confusingly written, and sometimes just plain wrong. Sure, go on the Internet, but don't forget to bring your skepticism with you. Just because it's online, doesn't mean it's true.

That said, here are some sites to hunt for facts that are more reliable than most.

Atlas Obscura. www.atlasobscura.com/

Encyclopaedia Britannica. www.britannica.com/

The Fact Site. www.thefactsite.com/

Funology: Trivia and Strange Facts. www.funology.com/trivia-and-strange-facts/

Lonely Planet. www.lonelyplanet.com/

National Geographic: Weird But True! https://kids.nationalgeographic.com/explore/adventure_pass/weird-but-true/

100 Interesting Facts about Practically Everything. www.rd.com/culture/interesting-facts/

Scholarpedia. www.scholarpedia.org/article/Main_Page

Snopes: The Internet's Definitive Fact-Checking Resource. www.thefactsite.com/

Index

A

Abaroa, Eduardo, 130
Africa, 14, 56. *see also* South Africa
    Beng people in, 78
    cell phone use in, 198
    father of cinema in, 158
    Fulani girls in, 78
    Herero people fashion in, 70
    matatu buses in, 186
    on Mercator projection
        world map, 31
    oompah day in, 132
    queah game in, 183
    San people of, 59
    Swahili language in, 62
    tribal twins view in, 77
    voodoo tradition in, 95
    Wak sky god folklore in, 69
Ahmadinejad, Mahmoud,
    height of, 45
Aïn Séfra, Algeria, 36
Amazon rainforest
    Pirahã language in, 61
    plants use in, 39
American Society for the
    Prevention of Cruelty to Animals
    (ASPCA), 115
animals, 22
Australia's platypus, 26
    Big Major Cay pigs, 26
    Lake Nakuru National Park
        flamingos, 27
    Mongolian Bankhar Dog Project,
        27
    Southeast Asia slow loris, 27
    Swiss protection laws for, 50
Apple, 12
Arafat, Yasser, height of, 45
ASPCA. *see* American Society for the
    Prevention of Cruelty to Animals
Australia
    aboriginal spiritual practices in,
        95
    bauxite-mining of, 13
    cockroach races in, 175
    "crocodile dive" in, 176
    election day of week in, 46
    micronations in, 43
    national symbol of, 22
    platypus in, 26
    potato law of, 51
    School of the Air in, 142
    two-party system in, 42
    Uluru rock formation in, 15

B

babies, newborn
    African tribes twins view of, 77
    Balinese culture concerning, 77
    outside napping of, 76
    Spanish devil's jump and, 77
    tossing of, 76
Bagram Air Force Base, Afghanistan,
    49
Bandaranaike, Sirimavo, 44
Bastoy Prison, Norway, 55
Becerra, Diego Felipe, 165
Belize, 113
    flag of, 17
    national bird of, 23
bin Barghash, Khalid, 48
birds
    as national symbols, 23
    urban adaptation of, 32
BitCoin, 21
Björnsson, Hafþór Júlíus, 178
Boko Haram, 103
Bonaparte, Napoleon, height of, 45
Bourdain, Anthony, 112
Brazil
    bauxite-mining of, 13
    Candomblé religion in, 94
    compulsory military service in, 48
    grading system in, 140
    hopscotch in, 180
    Jesus statue in, 15
    luta de galo game in, 181
    national dance of, 153, 157
    pride parades in, 135
    Saci Pererê folklore of, 68
Bruijn, Frank de, 192
bugs
    ant weight facts, 28
    dung beetles, 29
    killer bees, 29
    mosquitoes, 29
    titan beetle, 29

C

Canada
    election day of week in, 46
    fusion food in, 111
    Inunnguiniq, 79
    landmass of, 10
    maple syrup heist in, 53
    natural resources of, 13
    real place names in, 31

Ceauşescu, Nikolae, 45
celebrations, 82, 100, 120–121, 155
    Benin birthday years, 124
    Bolivian Dia del Mar as, 130
    Buddhist cham dances as, 133
    Crying Sumo Festival as, 122, 132
    fireworks in, 136–137
    flower parades as, 135
    Ghanaian oto use in, 125
    Grand Parade of the Marksmen
        as, 135
    India kite flying as, 126
    Jewish festival of Passover, 123
    largest firework shell in, 123, 137
    LGBTQ pride parades as, 135
    military parades as, 134
    Mongolian older birthday, 125
    oompah Africa as, 132
    Russian birthday traditions as,
        125
    second line parades as, 134
    Vietnamese Tet as, 124
Central America, Mayan ancestry in,
    56, 58
Chevalier, Maurice, 86
childhood
    Beng belief about, 78
    concept of, 78
    Fulani girls expectations in, 78
    Inuit of Canada responsibility in,
        79
    North Korean songbun
        impacting, 79
China, 11, 21
    bauxite-mining of, 13
    catch the dragon game in, 180
    cram schools in, 147
    Dragon Boat Festival in, 130
    ethnic groups in, 58
    Falun Gong ban in, 102
    fireworks invention in, 136
    Go game in, 183
    Iron Man 3 in, 158
    ling chi (slow slicing) in, 55
    meat-smuggling industry in, 53
    military parades in, 134
    New Year legend in, 128
    one time zone in, 72
    opera tradition in, 163
    panda nannies in, 149
    popular reality competition show
        in, 167
    proverb use in, 65
    reincarnation law of, 41, 50
    school naps in, 141

soccer invention in, 168
State Religious Affairs Bureau
Order #5 of, 41, 50
Taihang mountain tunnel in, 189
wrong friendship gifts in, 83
chocolate, true feeling and
obligation, 85
Christianopoulos, Dinos, 65
Churchill, Winston, height of, 45
Çiftçi, Bilgin, 52
City Montessori School, India, 139,
143
Clark, Joe, 111
climates
blood rain in, 36
Catatumbo River lightning
storms, 36
colored rains and causes in, 36
"fire whirl" in, 37
killer hail, 37
snow in hottest place on earth,
36
communication
African cell phone use for, 198
in ancient Greece, 184
digital, 184
iPhone 5 expense in, 198
Japan's cell and smartphone use
in, 199
nomophobia in, 199
on-hold music invention in, 199
phone facts in, 199
Cook, John, 91, 95
cooking, 108
bamboo uses for, 114
Māori traditions in, 114
pit ovens for, 114
turnspit and turnspit dogs use in,
115
crafts
kiffa beads in, 164
old year dolls as, 165
shadda weaving as, 164
street art or modern graffiti as,
165
crime, 161
"advance-fee fraud" as, 52
Canadian maple syrup heist as,
53
China's meat-smuggling industry
as, 53
Email scam as, 52
Spanish Prisoner con in, 52
Turkey's Provision 301 regarding,
52
Cuevas de Mármol, Chile, 34

D

Dalai Llama, 50
dance, 133
Capoeira as, 153, 157
categories of, 156
Cossack style, 156
Maasai warrior adumu as, 156
Macarena as, 157
tinikling as, 157
Dasht-e-Lut, Iran, temperature and
environment of, 25
Day, Willy, 84
death, 51, 188
Ghana fantasy coffins for, 89
Madagascar turning of bones
tradition in, 88
New Orleans cemeteries and jazz
funerals for, 89
Tibetan sky funerals for, 88
Democratic Republic of the Congo
(DRC), 140
"conflict mineral" of, 12
nationwide curriculum of, 145
Denmark, 17, 129, 141
Dessalines, Jean-Jacques, 17
dhebi a tugoin (flat disks), 56
dining etiquette
"clean plate" significance in, 118
cushions on floor in, 118
eating with hands in, 119
North Korean, 119
plate purity in, 119
sitting correctly as, 118
table and chair in, 118
Domitien, Elisabeth, 44
Doubleday, Abner, 171
Drake, Francis, 36
DRC. see Democratic Republic of the
Congo
drinks
bird nest soda as, 117
coffee and tea as, 116
fermented horse milk as, 116
seagull wine as, 116
snake wine as, 116
soda variations in, 117

E

East Antarctic Plateau, temperature
of, 25
ecosystems
cold deserts as, 33
coral reefs as, 33

Danakil Depression as, 32
sky islands as, 35
taiga as largest, 33
tropical rainforests as, 33
Egypt
Coptic Christian population in, 91
writ of protection in, 104
elderly people
ancient Rome and, 87
France's civil code regarding, 86
Ikaria island residents as, 75, 87
Inuit sacrifice myth about, 86
Japan's centenarians rate of, 86
Erdoğan, Recep Tayyip, 52
Ethiopia
boy to man bull jumping
ceremony in, 81
Gonder nickname in, 14
injera plate use in, 109
Jewish religion in, 93
Mursi tribe girls in, 56
ethnic groups
Central American Mayan ancestry
as, 56, 58
China's Hezhen population as, 58
in India, 59
Lacandon as, 58
San people of Africa as, 59

F

fashion, 80
Aymara women bowler hats as,
71
Bhutan nationwide dress code,
70
Herero people regarding, 70
shoe facts in, 71
Federation of Quebec Maple Syrup
Producers, 53
fireworks, 123
chemical compounds in, 136
facts about, 137
invention of, 136
pellet patterns in, 137
first ladies, 44
flags
of Belize, 17
of Denmark, 17
Haiti's creation of, 17
of Liechtenstein, 17
moon and, 17
on Mount Everest, 17
of Nepal, 16
Philippines bicolor, 17

Photo Credits

Front Cover: (central image) Art of Life/Shutterstock; (parrot) Passakorn Umpornmaha/Shutterstock; (Freedom Tower) William Perugini/Shutterstock; (cruise ship) NAN728/Shutterstock; (Statue of Liberty) Luciano Mortula - LGM/Shutterstock; (butterfly) Butterfly Hunter/Shutterstock; (ant) DrPAS/Thinkstock
Back Cover: (central image) sdecoret/Shutterstock; (pizza) danilsnegmb/Thinkstock; (desert sunset) tonda/Thinkstock; (cheetah) Saddako/Thinkstock; (Carnival reveler) filipefrazao/Thinkstock; (banknotes) Kenishirotie/Thinkstock

2–3: ideapixel/Shutterstock; **4–5:** Bartosz Hadyniak/Getty; **8–9:** ferrantraite/Getty; **9 (UP):** RLRRLRLL/Shutterstock; **9 (LO):** pandapaw/Shutterstock; **10 (UP):** simonlong/Getty; **10 (LO):** mariakraynova/Shutterstock; **11 (LE):** Naufal MQ/Getty; **11 (RT):** e X p o s e/Shutterstock; **12 (UP):** Steve Allen/Getty; **12 (LO):** hsagencia/shutterstock; **13 (UP LE):** James P. Jeff J Daly/Alamy Stock Photo; **13 (UP RT):** Galyna Andrushko/Shutterstock; **13 (LO LE):** tobkatrina/Shutterstock; **13 (LO RT):** Last Refuge/robertharding/Getty; **14 (LE):** Trevor Kittelty/Shutterstock; **14 (RT):** S-F/Shutterstock; **15 (UP):** R Gombarik/Shutterstock; **15 (CT):** Uwe Aranas/Shutterstock; **15 (LO):** Maarten Zeehandelaar/Shutterstock; **16 (UP):** Jiri Flogel/Shutterstock; **16 (LO):** Pawan Kawan/Shutterstock; **17 (UP):** Millenius/Shutterstock; **17 (LO):** Derek Brumby/Shutterstock; **18 (UP):** Charles Sturge/Alamy Stock Photo; **18 (CT):** Patrick Foto/Shutterstock; **18 (LO):** Cavan Images/Alamy Stock Photo; **19:** Isa Foltin/Getty; **20 (UP):** ManoAfrica/Getty; **20 (LO):** LMspencer/Shutterstock; **21 (UP LE):** Anestis Samourkasidis/Alamy Stock Photo; **21 (UP RT):** Mega Pixel/Shutterstock; **21 (LO):** AnnaGarmatiy/Shutterstock; **22 (UP):** Richard J Ashcroft/Shutterstock; **22 (LO):** Goran Bogicevic/Shutterstock; **23 (LE):** bleex/Getty; **23 (RT):** Juan Carlos Vindas/Getty; **24:** Delbars/Shutterstock; **24–25:** LightField Studios/Shutterstock; **25 (UP):** Pyty/Shutterstock; **25 (LO):** Gallinago_media/Shutterstock; **26 (UP):** BlueOrange Studio/Shutterstock; **26 (CT):** Nejron Photo/Shutterstock; **26 (LO):** Martin Pelanek/Shutterstock; **27 (UP):** Anna Om/Shutterstock; **27 (CT):** Lisa Parsons/Shutterstock; **27 (LO):** Seregraff/Shutterstock; **28 (UP):** iana kauri/Shutterstock; **28 (CT):** image jungle/Getty; **28 (LO):** DrPas/Getty; **29 (LE):** AbelBrata/Getty; **29 (RT):** DE AGOSTINI PICTURE LIBRARY/Getty; **30 (UP):** Have Camera Will Travel | Central & South America/Alamy Stock Photo; **30 (LO):** saiko3p/Shutterstock; **31 (LE):** RTimages/Shutterstock; **31 (RT):** mauinow1/Getty; **32 (UP):** Bachkova Natalia/Shutterstock; **32 (LO):** Faviel_Raven/Shutterstock; **33 (LE):** Hakbong Kwon/Alamy Stock Photo; **33 (RT):** ultramarinfoto/Getty; **34 (UP):** Alberto Loyo/Shutterstock; **34 (LO):** Incomel/Getty; **35 (UP):** StockdelD/Shutterstock; **35 (LO):** 1001slide/Getty; **36 (UP):** Tourism Ministry/Xinhua/Alamy Live News; **36 (CT):** Karim Bouchetata/Alamy Stock Photo; **36 (LO):** Alexey Belyaev/Shutterstock; **37 (UP):** Ion George/Shutterstock; **37 (LO):** Cathy Withers-Clarke/Shutterstock; **38 (UP):** faak/Shutterstock; **38 (LO):** imageBROKER/Alamy Stock Photo; **39 (UP):** FG Trade/Getty; **39 (LO):** GlebSStock/Shutterstock; **40:** Brian Kenney/Shutterstock; **40–41:** Janece Flippo/Shutterstock; **41 (UP):** Globe Turner/Shutterstock; **41 (LO):** Dima Moroz/Shutterstock; **42:** Travel India/Alamy Stock Photo; **43 (UP):** 3dfoto/Shutterstock; **43 (LO):** Aisha Sylvester Shutterstock; **44 (LE):** Paul Marriott/Alamy Stock Photo; **44 (RT):** Rob Crandall/Alamy Stock Photo; **45 (UP):** Classic Image/Alamy Stock Photo; **45 (LO):** Tinxi/Shutterstock; **46 (UP):** Niyazz/Shutterstock; **46 (LO):** Hanasaki/Shutterstock; **47 (UP):** NASA/Getty; **47 (LO):** Agung Parameswara/Getty; **48 (UP):** H. Mark Weidman Photography/Alamy Stock Photo; **48 (LO):** Royal Geographical Society/Getty; **49 (LE):** Benjamin Young/Alamy Stock Photo; **49 (RT):** PRESS LAB/Shutterstock; **50 (LE):** Fishy King/Shutterstock; **50 (RT):** Vangert/Shutterstock; **51 (UP):** Wolna/Shutterstock; **51 (LO):** EQRoy/Shutterstock; **51 (RT):** michaeljung/Shutterstock; **52 (UP):** eakkasit90/Shutterstock; **52 (LO LE):** Zabotnova Inna/Shutterstock; **52 (LO RT):** Barry King/Getty; **53:** Feng Yu/Getty; **54 (UP):** Boguslaw Mazur/Shutterstock; **54 (LO):** Chris Clor/Getty; **55 (UP):** seroma72/Shutterstock; **55 (LO):** Mehaniq/Shutterstock; **56 (LE):** Jorge Fernandez/Alamy Stock Photo; **56 (RT):** Michael Maslan/Contributor/Getty; **56–57:** szefei/Shutterstock; **58 (UP):** WENN Rights Ltd/Alamy Stock Photo; **58 (LO):** Yiming Chen/Getty; **59 (UP):** xavierarnau/Getty; **59 (LO):** imageBROKER/Alamy Stock Photo; **60 (UP):** Folio Images/Alamy Stock Photo; **60 (LO):** jarnogz/Getty; **61 (LE):** blickwinkel/Alamy Stock Photo; **61 (RT):** Silvestre Garcia - IntuitivoFilms/Getty; **62 (UP):** Minerva Studio/Shutterstock; **62 (LO):** hadynyah/Getty; **63 (LE):** Iakov Filimonov/Alamy Stock Photo; **63 (RT):** Juanmonino/Getty; **64:** Thanapon ch/Shutterstock; **65 (UP):** Olga Danylenko/Shutterstock; **65 (LO):** Romolo Tavani/Shutterstock; **66 (UP):** Pete Saloutos/Alamy Stock Photo; **66 (LO):** clumpner/Getty; **67 (UP):** ARCTIC IMAGES/Alamy Stock Photo; **67 (LO):** Pambudi Yoga Perdana/Shutterstock; **68 (UP):** Pat Maguet/Shutterstock; **68 (LO):** imagetico/Shutterstock; **69 (UP):** imageBROKER/Alamy Stock Photo; **69 (LO):** mrjo/Shutterstock; **70 (UP):** Deco/Alamy Stock Photo; **70 (LO):** robertharding/Alamy Stock Photo; **71 (UP):** Bartosz Hadyniak/Getty; **71 (RT):** Dani Simmonds/Alamy Stock Photo; **71 (LO):** hadynyah/Getty; **72 (UP):** HelloRF Zcool/Shutterstock; **72 (LO):** asikkk/Getty; **73 (UP):** Brenda Smith DVM/Shutterstock; **73 (LO):** AndreaAstes/Getty; **74:** Homo Cosmicos/Shutterstock; **74–75:** KonstantinChristian/Shutterstock; **75 (UP):** ivosar/Shutterstock; **75 (LO):** Makistock/Shutterstock; **76 (UP):** seirceil/Shutterstock; **76 (LO):** Nikhil Gangavane/Alamy Stock Photo; **77 (UP):** Tetra Images, LLC/Alamy Stock Photo; **77 (CT):** Lopolo/Shutterstock; **77 (LO):** Anders Ryman/Alamy Stock Photo; **78 (UP):** Danita Delimont/Alamy Stock Photo; **78 (LO):** Irene Abdou/Alamy Stock Photo; **79 (UP):** Blaine Harrington III/Alamy Stock Photo; **79 (LO):** Johner Images/Getty; **80 (UP):** iordani/Shutterstock; **80 (LO):** Ilya Rudzis/Shutterstock; **81:** Alberto Loyo/Shutterstock; **82:** Caiaimage/Trevor Adeline/Getty; **83 (UP):** View Apart/Shutterstock; **83 (LO):** Hinterhaus Productions/Getty; **83 (RT):** Radu Bercan/Shutterstock; **84 (UP):** Photo Spirit/Shutterstock; **84 (LO):** joan gravell/Alamy Stock Photo; **85 (LE):** KPG_Payless/Shutterstock; **85 (RT):** n_defender/Shutterstock; **86 (UP):** CroMary/Shutterstock; **86 (CT):** Education Images/Getty; **86 (LO):** Nikada/Getty; **87 (UP):** Steve Outram/Alamy Stock Photo; **87 (LO):** Massan/Shutterstock; **88 (UP):** travelib culture/Alamy Stock Photo; **88 (LO):** 7hanut/Shutterstock; **89 (UP):** Religious Images/UIG/Getty; **89 (LO):** Erika Goldring/Getty; **90–91:** SantiPhotoSS/Shutterstock; **91 (UP):** Park Ji Sun/Shutterstock; **91 (CT):** Martin Prochazkacz/Shutterstock; **91 (LT):** Stefano Buttafoco/Shutterstock; **92 (UP):** TripDeeDee Photo/Shutterstock; **92 (LO):** David South/Alamy Stock Photo; **93 (UP):** LiudmylaSupynska/Getty; **93 (LO):** She-Hulk/Shutterstock; **93 (RT):** VanderWolf Images/Getty; **94 (UP):** Luis Dafos/Alamy Stock Photo; **94 (LO):** Stefano Paterna/Alamy Stock Photo; **95 (LE):** clubfoto/Getty; **95 (UP):** Penny Tweedie/Alamy Stock Photo; **95 (RT):** Neil Farrin/Getty; **96 (UP):** Dmitry V. Petrenko/Shutterstock; **96 (LO):** DZarzycka/Getty; **97 (UP LE):** Alissa Everett/Alamy Stock Photo; **97 (UP RT):** Alissa Everett/Alamy Stock Photo; **97 (LO):** Tom Williams/Getty; **98 (UP):** Clemens Bilan/Getty; **98 (LO):** incamerastock/Alamy Stock Photo; **99 (UP):** Chris Clor/Getty; **99 (LO):** NASA/Getty; **100 (UP):** Partha Pal/Alamy Stock Photo; **100 (LO):** Sean Gallup/Getty; **101 (UP):** Mama Belle and the kids/Shutterstock; **101 (LO):** Alamy; **102 (UP):** Brendon Thorne/Getty; **102 (LO):** Miriam Reik/Alamy Stock Photo; **103 (LE):** Alvaro Puig/Shutterstock; **103 (RT):** david sanger photography/Alamy Stock Photo; **104 (UP):** Billion Photos/Shutterstock; **104 (LO):** Pongsakorn Nualchavee/Shutterstock; **105 (LE):** drbimages/Getty; **105 (RT):** cagi/Shutterstock; **106:** Oleg Elkov/Shutterstock; **106–107:** Igor Plotnikov/Shutterstock; **107:** Karaidel/Shutterstock; **108 (UP):** Shootdiem/Shutterstock; **108 (LO):** VadiCo/Shutterstock; **109 (UP):** Dereje/Shutterstock; **109 (LO):** Florin Gabriel/Shutterstock; **110 (UP):** Nungning20/Shutterstock; **110 (LO):** Dumitrescu Ciprian-Florin/shuttertock; **111 (UP):** Marlene Rounds/Getty; **111 (LO):** Stuart Dee/Getty; **112 (UP):** Mint Images Ltd/Alamy Stock Photo; **112 (LO):** Gestiafoto/Shutterstock; **113 (UP):** Olgysha/Shutterstock; **113 (CT):** Eric Isselee/Shutterstock; **113 (LO):** jeep2499/Shutterstock; **114 (UP):** Everything You Need/Shutterstock; **114 (LO):** James Nesterwitz/Alamy Stock Photo; **115:** Nadezhda V. Kulagina/Shutterstock; **116 (UP):** Rawpixel.com/Shutterstock; **116 (LO):** Nok Lek/Shutterstock; **117 (UP):** M. Unal Ozmen/Shutterstock; **117 (LO):** icosha/Shutterstock; **118 (UP):** Phil Hill/Alamy Stock Photo; **118 (LO):** urbanbuzz/Shutterstock; **119 (UP):** Jasmin Merdan/Getty; **119 (CT):** StockImageFactory.com/Shutterstock; **119 (LO):** ERIC LAFFORGUE/Alamy Stock Photo; **120 (UP):** Flavo Saru/Shutterstock; **120 (LO):** SAOWALAK SINGHAPAN/Shutterstock; **121 (UP):** Lotus Images/Shutterstock; **121 (CT):** MThanaphum/Shutterstock; **121 (LO):** Damian Tully/Alamy Stock Photo; **122:** YAY Media AS/Alamy Stock Photo; **122–123:** Melinda Nagy/Shutterstock; **123:** tomertu/Shutterstock; **124 (UP):** Pham Le Huong Son/Getty; **124 (LO):** Godong/Getty; **125 (UP):** Pixel-Shot/Shutterstock; **125 (CT):** Kathy deWitt/Alamy Stock Photo; **125 (LO):** Katiekk/Shutterstock; **126 (UP):** Sagase48/Shutterstock; **126 (LO):** AJP/Shutterstock; **127 (UP):** Ioana Catalina E/Shutterstock; **127 (LO):** Ellen Morgan/Alamy Stock Photo; **128 (UP):** Keren Su/China Span/Alamy Stock Photo; **128 (LO):** sahlan/Shutterstock; **129 (UP):** Aptyp_koK/Shutterstock; **129 (CT):** Adil Chelebiyev/Alamy Stock Photo; **129 (LO):** mauritius images GmbH/Alamy Stock Photo; **130 (UP):** Zoonar GmbH/Alamy Stock Photo; **130 (LO):** windmoon/Shutterstock; **131 (UP):** velirina/Shutterstock; **131 (LO):** edwin remsberg/Getty; **132 (UP):** Mahathir Mohd Yasin/Shutterstock; **132 (LO):** Thomas Dressler/Getty; **133 (UP):** ryosho/Shutterstock; **133 (LO):** Lucy Brown-loca4motion/Shutterstock; **134 (UP):** Rafael Ben-Ari/Alamy Stock Photo; **134 (LO):** CrackerClips Stock Media/shuttertock; **135 (UP):** blickwinkel/Alamy Stock Photo; **135 (CT):** allanw/Shutterstock; **135 (LO):** oscar garces/Shutterstock; **136 (UP):** anek.soowannaphoom/Shutterstock; **136 (LO):** ajt/Shutterstock; **137 (LE):** Kha Ngo/EyeEm/Getty; **137 (RT):** Patryk Kosmider/Shutterstock; **138:** Andre Nery/Shutterstock; **138–139:** Sangkhom Simma/Getty; **139 (UP):** Imagesbazaar/Getty; **139 (LO):** Jaws_73/Shutterstock; **140 (UP):** Katrina Wittkamp/Getty; **140 (LO):** Kichigin/Shutterstock; **141 (LE):** Mike Flippo/Shutterstock; **141 (RT):** Evening_T/Shutterstock; **142 (UP):** Jonas Gratzer/LightRocket/Getty; **142 (LO):** mark higgins/Shutterstock; **143 (UP):** Werli Francois/Alamy Stock Photo; **143 (LO):** Pongpachara Ratsameechand/Shutterstock; **144 (UP):** Eric Lafforgue/Alamy Stock Photo; **144 (LO):** Timothy Allen/Getty; **145 (UP):** Bill Bachmann/Alamy Stock Photo; **145 (LO):** Simon Rawles/Getty; **146 (UP):** PhotoAlto/James Hardy/Getty; **146 (LO):** Shoji Fujita/Getty; **147 (UP LE):** SG Studio/Shutterstock; **147 (UP RT):** Aurelie Marrier d'Unienville/Alamy Stock Photo; **147 (LO):** Brandon Fike/Shutterstock; **148 (UP):** Chad Ehlers/Getty; **148 (LO):** Milkovasa/Shutterstock; **149 (LE):** Emilie CHAIX/Getty; **149 (RT):** Eric Isselee/Shutterstock; **150 (UP):** baredbeast/Shutterstock; **150 (LO):** Christian Kober/Getty; **151 (LE):** Tom Gilks/Alamy Stock Photo; **151 (RT):** Justin Sullivan/Staff/Getty; **152:** Black Kings/Shutterstock; **152–153:** View Apart/Shutterstock; **152–153 (UP):** OSTILL is Franck Camhi/Shutterstock; **153:** Nicoleta Ionescu/Shutterstock; **154 (UP):** Pavel Filatov/Alamy Stock Photo; **154 (LO):** DOUGBERRY/Getty; **155 (LE):** Sean Gallup/Getty; **155 (RT):** Dmitry_Chulov/Getty; **156 (UP):** Delbars/iStock; **156 (LO):** A_Stepanov/Thinkstock; **157 (CT):** Tony Magdaraog/Shutterstock; **157 (UP):** OSTILL is Franck Camhi/Shutterstock; **157 (LO):** Vladislav T. Jirousek/Shutterstock; **158 (UP):** Iulian Dragomir/Alamy Stock Photo; **158 (LO):** ESB Professional/Shutterstock; **159 (LE):** Dinodia Photos/Alamy Stock Photo; **159 (RT):** Kristina Postnikova/Shutterstock; **160 (UP):** Daniel Jedzura/Shutterstock; **160 (LO):** David Turnley/Getty; **161 (UP):** Nicescene/Shutterstock; **161 (CT):** MonkeyTeam.ru/Shutterstock; **161 (LO):** Igor Kovalchuk/Shutterstock; **162:** Peter Treanor/Alamy Stock Photo; **163 (UP LE):** Christopher Y.C. Wong/Shutterstock; **163 (UP RT):** Bruno Passigatti/Shutterstock; **163 (LO):** Robert Estall photo agency/Alamy Stock Photo; **164 (UP):** The Picture Art Collection/Alamy Stock Photo; **164 (LO):** Oliver Blaise/Getty; **165 (UP):** Krzysztof Dydynski/Getty; **165 (LO):** Shanti Hesse/Getty; **166:** Tinxi/Shutterstock; **167 (UP):** graphbottles/Shutterstock; **167 (LO):** Jamaway/Alamy Stock Photo; **168 (UP):** Sovenko Artem/Shutterstock; **168 (LO):** maxim ibragimov/Shutterstock; **168–169:** Brocreative/Shutterstock; **169 (UP):** RTimages/Shutterstock; **169 (LO):** Africa Studio/Shutterstock; **170 (UP):** National Geographic Image Collection/Alamy Stock Photo; **170 (LO):** Javier Pierini/offset; **171 (UP):** Hindustan Times/Getty; **171 (CT):** RTimages/Shutterstock; **172 (UP):** Katiekk/Shutterstock; **172 (LO):** CRS PHOTO/Shutterstock; **173 (UP):** JASPERIMAGE/Shutterstock; **173 (LO LE):** Laszlo Mates/Shutterstock; **173 (LO):** OSTILL is Franck Camhi/Shutterstock; **174 (UP):** Richard Heathcote/Getty; **174 (LO):** wikipedia; **175 (UP):** Jonathan Wood/Getty; **175 (CT):** Somchai Som/Shutterstock; **175 (LO):** Yavuz Sariyildiz/Shutterstock; **176 (UP):** IULIZU/Shutterstock; **176 (LO):** Philip Waller/Alamy Stock Photo; **177 (UP):** Delmas Lehman/Shutterstock; **177 (LO):** JIANG HONGYAN/Shutterstock; **178 (UP):** Gilbert Carrasquillo/Getty; **178 (LO):** Alex Kravtsov/Shutterstock; **179 (UP):** freestyle images/Shutterstock; **179 (LO):** Aflo Co. Ltd./Alamy Stock Photo; **180 (UP):** NadyaEugene/Shutterstock; **180 (LO):** Mr. Ratchacrit Nakkhonok/Shutterstock; **181 (UP):** Eric Isselee/Shutterstock; **181 (LO):** Paula Bronstein/Getty; **182 (UP):** Harismoyo/Shutterstock; **182 (LO):** CatherineLProd; **183 (UP):** BornMedia/Shutterstock; **183 (LO):** Nataliia Dvukhimenna/Shutterstock; **184:** Beerpixs; **184–185:** Beerpixs/Getty; **185–186:** Everett Historical/Shutterstock; **186 (UP):** Philou1000/Shutterstock; **186 (LO):** imagegallery2/Alamy Stock Photo; **187 (UP):** Wollertz/Shutterstock; **187 (LO LE):** Eduard Valentinov/Shutterstock; **187 (LO RT):** ilozavr/Shutterstock; **188 (UP):** imageBROKER/Alamy Stock Photo; **188 (LO):** cyo bo/Shutterstock; **189 (UP):** RodionY/Shutterstock; **189 (LO):** Yuangeng Zhang/Shutterstock; **190 (UP):** Gerner Thomsen/Alamy Stock Photo; **190 (LO):** Olga Danylenko/Shutterstock; **191 (UP):** David Ball/Alamy Stock Photo; **191 (LO):** shan.shihan/Getty; **192 (UP):** mariakraynova/Shutterstock; **192 (LO):** Hottug/Firebox/Solent News/Shutterstock; **193 (UP):** Salvacampillo/Shutterstock; **193 (LO):** Em Campos/Shutterstock; **194 (UP):** Tupungato/Shutterstock; **194 (LO):** IZO/Shutterstock; **195 (UP):** Vibrant Image Studio/Shutterstock; **195 (LO):** Yuriy Vlasenko/Shutterstock; **196 (UP):** Natsuki Sakai/AFLO/Alamy Stock Photo; **196 (LO):** agolndr/Shutterstock; **197 (UP):** muratart/Shutterstock; **197 (LO):** Cherries/Shutterstock; **198 (UP):** National Geographic Image Collection/Alamy Stock Photo; **198 (LO):** nito/Shutterstock; **199 (UP LE):** F-Stop boy/Shutterstock; **199 (UP RT):** Quality Stock Arts/Shutterstock; **199 (LO):** Antonio Guillem/Shutterstock